It's Not Over 'till The Barren Woman Sings

Paul Scanlon

Abundant Life Publishing

British Library Cataloguing in Publication Data
A record for this book is available from the British Library

ISBN 0-9538516-0-5

Typeset and cover design by
Creative I, The Barn, Hawkesworth Lane, Guiseley, Leeds, LS20 8HD

Published by:
Abundant Life Publishing
Abundant Life Centre
Wapping Road
Bradford
BD3 0EQ

Dedication

I dedicate this book to our four beautiful daughters Charlotte, Ruth, Bethan and Esther. I love you all tons - and whatever you do, don't live an ordinary life!

Acknowledgements

To Stephen and Kay Matthew, a big thank you for the hours of editorial input to this book. Thank you for your partnership in our dream and your friendship with Glenda and I.

To Charlotte, thank you for believing in this book and especially for encouraging me to keep going when it got tough. I promise to do the same for you when you write your book.

Contents

CHAPTER ONE

It's Not Over 'til The Barren Woman Sings

It's Not Over 'til The Barren Woman Sings

'"Sing, O barren woman, you who never bore a child; burst into song, shout for joy, you who were never in labour; because more are the children of the desolate woman than of her who has a husband," says the Lord. "Enlarge the place of your tent, stretch your tent curtains wide, do not hold back; lengthen your cords, strengthen your stakes. For you will spread out to the right and to the left; your descendants will dispossess nations and settle in their desolate cities."' (Isaiah 54:1)

Who is the 'barren woman' spoken of in these verses? And what's not over until she sings? As we will see, the barren woman could be anyone; and what's 'not over' until she sings is her chance of becoming pregnant.

Isaiah 54 is not a scripture about gender; the barren woman is a prophetic image used to describe the

> The barren woman is a prophetic image used to describe the spiritual barrenness of Israel

spiritual barrenness of Israel at that time in her history. Israel had failed to walk in the covenant promises of God and Isaiah was once again calling them back from the brink of disaster towards a restoration of fruitfulness. So the barren woman can be typical of a nation, a church or a relationship. She can be a marriage, an individual, a ministry or a calling. She can even be a pastor or a leader. The barren woman image could represent us all at some stage of life.

The curse of barrenness

It is important to understand that when we use the word 'barren' in our modern western society, it does not have the same connotations as it had in the time, culture and nation that we are dealing with in Isaiah 54. Barrenness was a curse. It was considered a curse to be unable to have children because children were a blessing from God. Not to have a fruitful womb and be able to have children was therefore a shameful condition to be in. A closed womb was an unbearable stigma for a woman to carry. It was invariably viewed as a judgement from God for sin either in her life, or in the life of her family ancestry.

Do you remember Michal, David's wife the daughter of Saul? She was struck barren by God for despising David's liberty when he danced before the Lord (2 Samuel 6:23). It's not surprising therefore that barrenness carried such a stigma. You see, from the beginning fruitfulness was God ordained; it was written into the DNA of creation that everything should reproduce after its kind. Every living thing that God created in Genesis 1 was commissioned to keep on creating. All that God gave was designed to keep on giving. Every fruit had within it the next generation of fruit in seed form. The animals, the fish of the sea and the birds of the air were all empowered to reproduce. And to Adam and Eve, the first church, he said I want you to be fruitful, to increase in number, to multiply and fill the earth (Genesis1:28).

> **Life is a sacred stewardship to be managed and fruitful reproduction its ultimate goal.**

Life is inherently reproductive. Life without reproduction is a stagnant pool, a dead end of locked up resources. Life will always reproduce after its kind and any organism which refuses to do so, by denying its facilities for transmission, commits a breach of trust. Nowhere in creation was life given as a possession to be enjoyed. It is rather a sacred stewardship to be managed and fruitful reproduction its ultimate goal.

The barren fig tree

The account of the barren fig tree in Matthew 21:18 is a shocking description of how seriously God views a lack of fruitfulness:

'Early in the morning, as he went on his way back to the city, he was hungry. Seeing a fig tree by the road he went up to it but found nothing on it except leaves. Then he said to It: "May you never bear fruit again." Immediately the tree withered. When the disciples saw this they were amazed. "How did the tree wither so quickly?" they asked.'

No doubt the disciples viewed this action of Jesus as a little strange and somewhat extreme; after all it was only a fig tree. To Jesus, however, it was far more than a fig tree; it was a parable of an unfulfilled trust, it was receiving life without passing it on. The fig tree was a creational violation. It drew people to itself in the expectation of receiving

> It was receiving life without passing it on.

fruit, only to send them away hungry and empty. In this fig tree Jesus saw pictured the barrenness of a legalistic, pharisaical religion to which he spoke the same stinging rebuke. Today, Jesus comes to his church looking for the fruit of our union with him. But sadly in many cases, only to find another barren fig tree.

In Luke 13:16-18 we find another insight into God's view of barrenness:

'Then he told this parable: "A man had a fig tree, planted in his vineyard, and he went to look for fruit on it, but did not find any. So he said to the man who took care of the vineyard, 'For three years now I've been coming to look for fruit on this fig tree and haven't found any. Cut it down! Why should it use up the soil?'

"'Sir,' the man replied, 'leave it alone for one more year, and I'll dig around it and fertilize it. If it bears fruit next year, fine! If not, then cut it down.'"

We are presented with three major, and very fundamental principles, about how God views both productivity and barrenness. First, there is a legitimate expectation of fruitfulness from the owner: 'For three years I have been looking for fruit on this tree.' Secondly, there is a refusal on the owner's part to put up with the continued barrenness: 'Cut it down.' Then thirdly, he initiates the removal of the tree so that the soil can be used by another plant that would make better use of it: 'Cut it down; it should not be using up the good soil with nothing to show for it.'

Why then do we sometimes feel so guilty about expecting fruitfulness from people in our churches? Why do we put up with bad attitude, poor performance and lack of productivity? Why do we feel so troubled about uprooting people or things, when we know full well that if we afforded the same opportunity to another person, they would thrive in the rich soil of opportunity that proved so infertile to the first person? I believe it is because we haven't yet made up our minds about barrenness. We don't feel what God feels about it and we therefore don't view it as God views it.

The nature of barrenness

Barrenness brings huge psychological and emotional baggage with it. It moves into our inner world, unpacks its deadly luggage and digs in like an illegal squatter. Barrenness, like a cancer, begins to destroy us from the inside out; paralysing creativity and eroding self worth, it pushes itself into every area of our life. This evil squatter attacks our mind and will, filling our confession with the language of lack and defeat. Our daily routines and relationships become progressively overwhelmed with the vice-like grip of unfruitfulness. Barren people begin to keep company with other barren people, obtaining small comfort from discovering that someone else is even more barren than they are.

> Barren people begin to keep company with other barren people, obtaining small comfort from discovering that someone else is even more barren than they are.

Such a jailer does not release his prisoners easily or without a fight. The only way out is to break out. Hell itself resists the breaking free of the barren into the outside world of increase and productivity. If the devil can't stop us going to heaven, he will settle for ensuring we are unproductive, barren and contained while on our way there. If he can't stop the seeds of fruitfulness being sown, he will seek to abort the harvest by convincing us that barrenness is an irreversible, terminal condition for which there is no cure.

> We must abandon our theologies of 'consolidation' and 'quality rather than quantity' which are nothing more than excuses for our own barrenness.

Sadly for many, the effort required to break free from a barren life seems too high a price to pay. But the truth is that there is no price too great for living life as God intended it to be. Child of God, you need to know that fruitfulness, enlargement and increase are your God given rights in every aspect of your life.

At the outset of this book, I want to establish that barrenness is never an option for God's people. We must abandon our theologies of 'consolidation' and 'quality rather than quantity' which are nothing more than excuses for our own barrenness.

Only when we feel what God feels about barrenness will we commit to breaking its grip on our lives and churches. And only then can the enlargement of Isaiah 54:2 become ours.

God's cycle of life

The Hebrew people were an agricultural people. They worked the land and understood the principles of seedtime and harvest intimately. They understood that life operates in an endless cycle of giving and receiving; a cycle started by God, which can only be broken by something or someone refusing to play their part in passing on the life they have received.

Nowhere is this concept better demonstrated than in 1 Chronicles 29 where King David initiated the greatest offering ever received. This offering was even more incredible because it was an 'over and above' offering. David had already made full provision for Solomon's temple years earlier (1 Chronicles 22:1-5). The motivation for this 'more than enough' offering therefore sprang, not from the external need, but from an internal and overwhelming desire to give and keep on giving. It's an Old Testament

> This kind of giving is rare because the energy for the giving does not come from the leadership but from the people

example of what the apostle Paul calls 'the grace of giving' (2 Corinthians 8:7). This kind of giving is rare because the energy for the giving does not come from the leadership persuading or encouraging people to give, but rather from the people themselves who are desperate to be part of God's life-giving cycle. They have moved from just giving to a specific need and are responding to a revelation of the bigger picture.

Needs do require money to satisfy them but it is always a vision of the bigger picture that moves people to give on this scale. They knew the much needed temple would cost a fortune, but the vision of God dwelling in the midst of his people in appropriate splendour motivated them to give, and keep on giving. When this grace of giving grips people, they eventually have to be restrained from giving anymore! This is what happened here with David and with Moses when he took the offering for the Tabernacle:

'The people continued to bring freewill offerings morning after morning. So the craftsman who were doing the work went to Moses and said the people are bringing more than enough for doing the work. Then Moses gave an order and they sent word throughout the camp, 'No man or woman is to bring anything else as an offering for the sanctuary.' And so the people were restrained from bringing any more because what they already had was more than enough to do all the work' (Exodus 36:3-7).

In the midst of the Temple offering, King David said, *'But who am I and who are my people that we should be able to give as generously as this. Everything comes from you and we have given you only what has come from your hand.' (1 Chronicles 29:14).* What a perfect description of God's cycle of life! Everything we have comes from God, and what comes from God must be kept in circulation by us passing it on to one another. Herein lies the antidote to barrenness in your life, church, marriage, family, friendships, business or ministry. The antidote is to continually pass on what you are receiving from God.

> The antidote is to continually pass on what you are receiving from God.

Dodo or rabbit?

Think about it. Why are some species plentiful and others, like the dodo, extinct? The answer is simply that some stay in the reproductive cycle of life and others, usually through human interference, are prevented from staying in God's cycle of life. The truth is that if anything stays in God's cycle of life, receiving life and passing it on, the potential for increase and productivity is without measure. Rabbits, chickens, rats and mice are all proof of this. And if you keep your life in God's cycle of life, then there is no limit to your increase.

I recall God once telling me to send money to a Pastor at the other side of town who I hardly knew. For me it was a small step of obedience; for him it was no doubt an absolute miracle of answered prayer. However, the whole episode left me a little confused. Why did God need me to send money to a stranger across town when he was leading a good church, was loved by his people and gave good teaching? Doubtless he also had close friends and maybe even family in town. I will never forget what God told me, 'I asked you to do it because I couldn't find anyone around him who was operating in my cycle of life.'

In other words, if God wants to get something to someone, he starts by finding someone within their immediate network of relationships who is operating in his cycle of life - someone who both receives and passes on. If he can't find anyone, God will then widen the search until he finds someone who will simply obey and do it. This helps us to understanding why the trail of God's provision is so often complex and meandering.

> God only has to do it mysteriously because the non-mysterious solution was not an option.

Ultimately it can only come through God's facilitators of life as opposed to the many withholders of his life. We often observe that 'God works in mysterious ways,' but I am sure that in many cases God only has to do it mysteriously because the non-mysterious solution was not an option. There were simply insufficient people available who were living and operating in his wonderful cycle of life.

To conclude this opening chapter, I simply want to challenge you about your own life. Is your life barren? Do you feel unproductive or unfruitful in your relationships, friendships and ministry? Do you feel dry and barren in your gift or calling? Are you barren in health, joy, creativity or success? And most importantly, are you operating in God's reproductive cycle of life?

Whatever area of your life you feel may be best described as barren, I have got good news for you. It can all change! However, the way to bring about this change may be quite a surprise. But you have nothing to lose and everything to gain by reading on, so lets go to chapter two.

CHAPTER TWO

God's Counsel to Barren People

God's Counsel to Barren People

Let's now examine the seemingly insensitive counsel which God gives to this barren woman. You will recall that she represents spiritual barrenness of any kind. Basically, God requires four responses from her. First he says, 'Sing O barren woman.' Secondly, 'Burst into song.' Thirdly, 'Shout for joy,' and fourthly, 'Enlarge your place.' What strange counsel this would appear to be! None of these actions are the responses you would expect from an unproductive, dry or stagnant people.

Most of us would not want the job of telling someone who we knew was going through a spiritually dry and unproductive patch, to burst into song, shout for joy or start making room for expansion. Rather than 'Sing O barren woman,' most of us would be saying, 'Pray O barren woman.' We are more likely to say, 'Burst into tears' and 'Shout with frustration,' than 'Burst into song' and 'Shout for joy.' We certainly wouldn't be saying, 'Now is the time to expand to make room for all the increase that's coming.' Instead we would probably be advising them not to do anything too rash, but to take it easy until this depression lifts, to play it safe.

God views everything from completion

There is something we all need to know about God, something so fundamental to our understanding of him that if we miss it, we will forever struggle with his apparent insensitivity to our problems: God views everything from completion.

God is already at the end of our lives looking back in time to where we are now. God is watching our lives like a man watching the 'Match of the Day' highlights who already knows the score. He knows the end from the beginning. He is immune from process. God doesn't have to wait to see what happens; he doesn't need things to develop before he knows the outcome. Did it ever occur to you that nothing ever occurs to God? God has no tomorrow and no yesterday; he just is. If God were writing the book of your life and it had a thousand pages, he would start with page number one thousand, write that page, and then move backwards writing every page from a completion point of view. As the Psalmist says: '*All the days ordained for me were written in your book before one of them came to be.*' (Psalm 139:16)

> Did it ever occur to you that nothing ever occurs to God?

From God's point of view we are like actors performing a pre-written script; there are surprises for us but no suprises for the scriptwriter. God looked at a depressed Gideon and saw greatness. At his first encounter with him, God addressed him from completion: *'The Lord is with you mighty warrior' (Judges 6:12)*. There was nothing about Gideon that even hinted he was a mighty warrior, yet only a short time later that is exactly what he was. God had already seen 'a short time later' and addressed Gideon from his future, not his present or his past.

God looked at a barren couple in their nineties called Abram and Sara and spoke to them about their children, which would be so numerous, no one would be able to count them. Both

> Catching a glimpse of the completion of our life when all we can see is today, seems hilariously funny!

Abram and Sara laughed at the prospect of starting a family and having kids, because catching a glimpse of the completion of our life when all we can see is today, seems hilariously funny! Abraham fell face down; he laughed and said to himself, *'Will a son be born to a man a hundred years old? Will Sarah bear a child at the age of ninety?' (Genesis 17:17)* The answer, of course, was yes!

God gives completion a name

The apostle Paul wrote that, *'God calls things that are not as though they were' (Romans 4:17).* Only someone who is able to see into the future can define the present in the light of it. God looked thousands of years ahead into our day, saw Abram's spiritual offspring and then changed his name in the light of it. Abram, which means 'exalted father' became Abraham, which means 'father of many nations.' For the following twelve years Abraham, with no children to his name, had to live with being called 'father of many children!'

Does God ever speak to you privately as if you were someone else? Does he speak to you about things you have never done, places you have never been, and people you have never met? Then don't be resistant or confused, just go with the flow. God is calling things in your life that 'are not,' as though they have already happened, because from God's perspective, they have.

'You will be Peter'

When Jesus looked at the young man brought to him by his brother Andrew, he saw more than anyone else present. He addressed him from a completion perspective and said, 'You are Simon,' which means 'reed like.' 'But you will be called Peter,' which means 'rock like' (John 1:42). From that moment on Jesus only ever related to Peter from a completion perspective.

No matter how things went or how low Peter seemed to get, God always saw his life from completion. When Peter denied Jesus three times and then ran out into the night weeping bitterly, he doubtless thought his life and ministry were over. But Luke's Gospel tells us that at the very moment of his third denial, while the rooster crowed, Jesus turned and looked straight at him (Luke 22:61). I do not believe it was a look of disappointment, judgement or betrayal, but rather one that said, 'Hold steady Peter the rock; I have already seen you reaching thousands on the day of Pentecost and this moment of denial must not be allowed to stop your destiny unfolding.'

Perhaps at this time in your life you feel that God would never want to use you again because of some failure or mistake on your part. When we think this way, we are treating God like a mere human being; like someone who needs time to recover from the effects of our betrayal or sin, in order to regain his trust in us. There may be people in your life right now, who at some time in the past hurt you. At the time, you probably thought you could never be friends with them again. But now, months or years later, you seem closer to them than ever. Well, imagine knowing back then exactly how things would turn out later and how much easier that knowledge would have made the whole situation. Now multiply that a few million times and you will be a little closer to understanding how God views everything about our lives.

God calls unsaved people harvest

When Jesus looked at the crowds following him - the thousands of lost, hopeless and aimless people - he saw something that no one else saw, he saw a harvest. *'When he saw the crowds he had compassion on them, because they were harassed and helpless like sheep without a shepherd. Then he said to his disciples, 'The harvest is plentiful but the workers are few. Ask the lord of the harvest, therefore, to send out workers into his harvest field.' (Matthew 9:36-38)*

Jesus didn't just see the present massive need, he saw the future potential of those people. He saw future apostles, evangelists, doctors, politicians, businessmen and so on, because 'harvest' is a completion word. When a farmer looks out across his ripe fields he doesn't just see ripe crops or even bread for the hungry, he sees the potential harvest of a brand new Mercedes and his wife sees a diamond ring! The farmer firstly has the harvest in view, he sees the pay off, and thus is motivated to work backwards from that perspective to plough, prepare the ground, sow his seed and gather a harvest.

When God first looked at our lives he saw the harvest. He saw

> He doesn't just see ripe crops or even bread for the hungry, he sees the potential harvest of a brand new Mercedes and his wife sees a diamond ring!

the pay off as being the useful vessels we would become to him and his kingdom. When God saved us he saw all we are doing for him today and everything we are about to do for him tomorrow. Remember, '*God calls things that are not as though they are*' (Romans 4:17). That's why God calls the unsaved a useful harvest.

Combine harvesters

About a year ago we started our bus ministry, which brings people from some of the most deprived parts of our inner city to the Church campus. We bus in hundreds of people every week. These wonderful people have taught me, once again, to look beyond the incredible needs or immediate problems that many bring with them, to the potential harvest within each of their lives. Every week I look out across the congregation and see new people who have ridden our buses and I see future pastors, evangelists, sportsmen and women, business men and women, politicians, musicians, youth workers, kids church workers, new bus pastors, and so much more. We call our buses 'combine harvesters' because every week they go out into the city bringing in God's harvest. Anybody can drive a bus, but only a farmer at harvest time needs a combine harvester; so that's what we sometimes call our buses. By so doing, we keep God's perspective in view.

I am learning to view people from completion and then to minister to them from that perspective. It has transformed my preaching and drawn an amazing response from the people. I have realised that big thinking starts with seeing people bigger than they see themselves. Then, through an empowering culture, drawing that greatness out

> **Big thinking starts with seeing people bigger than they see themselves.**

of them. People love being viewed from completion, they feel inspired to become what completion calls them.

Understanding this principle will give us a greater insight into Isaiah 54:1. God looked at this barren woman of Israel and, because he saw enlargement and dominion in her future, could say from a completion perspective: 'Sing O barren woman, burst into song and shout for joy, because you are going to birth more people and conquer more cities than you could ever imagine.'

God refuses to get down into our mess and negativity. He will enter our present, but only from our future or not at all. We may want someone to sympathise with us and invite others to our pity party, because misery loves company, but God will not be there. You need to know that the 'First law of Holes' is that if you're in one, you should stop digging! God may come to

> He will enter our present, but only from our future or not at all.

your hole, but he won't bring a shovel with him, he will throw you down a rope. That rope will often appear in the form of an act of obedience; something which God requires from us in order to break our own wrong pattern of response to the circumstances which surround us.

God can speak to barren people about singing and shouting for joy because he sees what's coming next. So, determine never to be offended by God's apparent insensitivity to your problem. He knows something you don't, has been where you are going, and has seen what you are about to see. God has already rejoiced over victories yet to be accomplished through your life. We see only a part, but God sees the whole picture. We are

> The 'First law of Holes' is ... stop digging!

trying to piece together the jigsaw puzzle, but God has got the box lid with the full picture on it!

Singing is your initiative

Singing requires something from you, praying requires something from God. Surely it would have made more sense to counsel the barren woman of Isaiah 54:1 to 'Pray O barren woman' rather than sing. But praying puts the initiative for change with God, whereas I believe with all my heart that the only way to break the stranglehold of barrenness in our lives and churches, is to take the initiative on ourselves. And that is what singing does.

Jail house rock

The Psalmist declared that God *'Leads forth the prisoners with singing' (Psalm 68:6)*. Singing is the Christian's equivalent to the Monopoly game's 'Get out of Jail Free' card! Singing prisoners are a nightmare to a jailer; they stir up hope in other prisoners as they draw from an invisible source which, as is all too evident, cannot be imprisoned. Singing prisoners are dangerous, they can incite riots, upset regimes, break yokes and inspire the spirit of freedom in a place where freedom does not belong.

Paul and Silas were once severely beaten and thrown into a filthy stinking jail

> Singing requires something from you, praying requires something from God.

cell. Their hands were chained and their feet put in stocks. They received no medical attention, replacement clothing or a bed on which to recover from their beating. And worst of all, they had done nothing illegal to merit any of this. They had simply obeyed the call of God to go to Macedonia and help someone that Paul saw in a vision. There had been no trial, they had no release date, and their human rights had been violated. They could not telephone a lawyer or contact a friend to post bail for them. I point all this out to help you grasp what an awful and frightening situation they were in.

Having set the scene a little and attempted to understood the terror of this nightmare, what we next read becomes all the more incredible:

'About midnight Paul and Silas were praying and singing hymns to God, and the other prisoners were listening to them. Suddenly there was such a violent earthquake that the foundations of the prison were shaken. At once all the prison doors flew open and everybody's chains came loose.' (Acts 16:25-26)

Paul and Silas were praying, which is what we would expect. But it is what they did next that's astonishing. They were praying 'and singing.' Yes, singing! Talk about 'Sing O barren woman!' This was the lowest, most barren point of their lives. They had gone to Philippi in response to a vision from God, had seen no great breakthrough, no great miracles and no revival. And for their trouble been thrown into this terrible jail. Yet at the darkest hour of midnight, in physical agony, they struck up a duet of praise to God - and the original 'Jail House Rock' took place!

We would all have prayed but we would not all have sung. Yet I believe that it was the singing that triggered the earthquake, not the praying. Despite your prayers many situations refuse to change. Perhaps it's because the only person that can do anything about it is you, and singing requires something from you. Singing doesn't change the situation, it changes you in the situation and gives God something to work with. Singing doesn't release enlargement and fruitfulness to you, it releases you to it. Singing shifts the authority and control from our external jailers, back to our inner man. The moment you take authority in a situation, is the moment you break an imprisonment over your life. Even though nothing may appear to change outwardly the foundation for change is now in place.

The old Negro Spiritual songs sprang from a refusal to allow slavery to break their spirit and kept alive the hope of freedom for generations. Black South Africans sang songs of freedom while still suffering

> Singing doesn't change the situation, it changes you in the situation and gives God something to work with.

under the oppression of an evil apartheid system. Thousands of Christian martyrs who were subjected to unimaginable torture throughout the centuries sang songs of freedom and deliverance at the hands of their torturers.

A singing prisoner is not a prisoner, he is an oasis of freedom in a place of bondage. Once you lose your song you lose your joy. And once your joy is gone there is no more immunity to the creeping infection of sterility and barrenness.

We will return to this prison scene in the next chapter, but for now I want you to notice one more thing. Not only Paul and Silas' chains fell off, everyone else's did too. It was not just their cell door that flew open, all of them did! Your song of freedom, expressed by your refusal to conform to a barren and containing environment, is about more than you alone. Many out there are waiting to be liberated from their stinking cell of containment and bondage, and we are the liberation bringers. By our song and through our liberty we bring a message of hope and heavenly liberation to the barren everywhere.

> A singing prisoner is not a prisoner, he is an oasis of freedom in a place of bondage.

Thermometer or thermostat?

Are you a thermometer or a thermostat? One simply tells you what the current temperature is while the other actually sets the temperature around it. Paul and Silas refused to just give a thermometer reading of their situation. They decided to re-set the temperature by becoming a thermostat in their environment.

Which one are you? How much of the way you think, feel and do is governed by what is going on around you, or by what people are saying about you? Are you happy when things are going well and sad when things are going badly? Are your ups and downs determined by the circumstantial climate around you? Do certain types of people completely dominate your personality and moods? If so, you are a thermometer.

When the Hebrew nation were taken captive to Babylon, unlike Paul and Silas, they were completely controlled by the environment of their captivity:

'By the rivers of Babylon we sat and wept when we remembered Zion. There on the poplars we hung our harps, for there our captors asked us for songs, our tormentors demanded songs of joy. They said, 'Sing us one of the songs of Zion.' How can we sing the songs of the Lord while in a foreign land?' (Psalm 137:1-4)

'How can we sing the songs of the Lord while living in a foreign land?' The answer is simple, by not letting the foreign land live in us. We must take control of our inner environment and let it set the temperature of our lives, whatever our external circumstances. We then become a thermostat, a marker of what the external temperature should be. And the way we then live will change the temperature around us. I believe the church should be the 'thermostat' of a nation not its government, business community, dictators or army. The church of God should be determining the moral, ethical, economic and spiritual climate of our towns and cities.

> The church should be the 'thermostat' of a nation not its government, business community, dictators or army.

What is the current temperature of your life and where did it come from? I get weary of hearing believers say, 'It's really tough, I'm the only Christian at my work place.' Or, 'I'm the only Christian in my class or neighbourhood.' That's wonderful, God has placed you there to bring a new climate to that environment. They have had winter for too long, go and bring God's springtime to them. Stop hanging your harp on the poplar tree and get singing!

CHAPTER THREE

Reverse
the curse

Reverse the curse

Any curse can be reversed, whether it be a curse of sickness, lack, poverty or even death. God can reverse anything. It's not over until God says it's over. Have you given up on a call, ministry, relationship or gift? Well don't, because God can reverse it. He can bring back anything into great fruitfulness. Never give up hope, because God sometimes waits for a thing to die before he steps in to reverse it.

The Law of Cause and Effect

Have you ever noticed that many preachers skip right over Isaiah 54 verse one and start reading at verse two? Admittedly, all the good stuff to talk about appears to be in verse two: 'Enlarge the place of your tent, stretch your tent curtains wide, do not hold back; lengthen your cords and strengthen your stakes, for you will spread out to the right and to the left.' But verse two follows verse one for an important reason, namely that they have a 'cause and effect' relationship. The cause is the action in verse one, and the effect is the potential enlargement of verse two. In other words, there can be no enlargement until barrenness is first dealt with. The cause of reaping is sowing, the cause of momentum is impetus, and the cause of harvest is seedtime. It is always important to know whether you are dealing with the cause or the effect in any given situation.

I have visited many churches that are not growing, but much prayer for growth goes on. Obviously they think that prayer causes numerical growth, but prayer alone is not the biblical cause of numerical growth. Appropriate effort is the cause of growth; ask any farmer about soil, seed and harvest and he will heartily confirm it. Harvest is an effect and not a cause. So, if we can identify the cause of the effect that we want, then all things become possible. In other words, we can have whatever we know how to cause.

I have been in many meetings where someone has prophesied, 'Enlarge the place of your tent, stretch your tent curtains wide' over the church. I have talked with pastors who are claiming these same verse as their church promise. I have seen many a church banner or poster in church buildings, with 'Enlarge the place of your tent' emblazoned across it. In recent years there have been a number of popular Christian songs on the theme of 'Enlarging the place of your tent' sung every week in churches across the world. Yet the

> Harvest is an effect and not a cause, we can have whatever we know how to cause.

simple truth has been that many churches, pastors and leaders who have claimed this promise have seen little or no enlargement in their city, church or personal lives. Why?

Because 'Enlarge the place of your tent' is not a promise - it is a command. We cannot claim a command we can only obey it. And we can only obey it if we first remove all hindrances to our obedience.

> 'Enlarge the place of your tent' is not a promise - it is a command. We cannot claim a command we can only obey it.

So, Isaiah 54 verse one is the cause of Isaiah 54 verse two. It is the key to the door through which we enter and possess the territory of verse two. Therefore, unless we first deal with barrenness we cannot have enlargement. We may sing and prophesy about enlargement but if our life is not causing enlargement, it is not going to happen.

Some of the most barren churches I have either visited or become aware of, are the most expectant of enlargement. Yet they have not realised that making it happen demands an all out war on barrenness. If our churches are barren in friendliness to visitors, then we can forget enlargement. If our churches are barren in friendships with unsaved people, then no amount of claiming enlargement will make any difference.

If our administration is barren of excellence, then we can forget enlargement. If our preaching is barren in its relevance to the practical issues of life, then we can forget enlargement.

It is not enough for me to preach enlargement in the pulpit but to allow barrenness in church departments. It is not enough to have the public language of enlargement and the private acceptance of barrenness. Both anti-barrenness and pro-enlargement must become our personal and corporate culture. Not just an emphasis and not simply a structure but our very culture, essence and DNA.

The law of reversal

To reverse a law you must apply an opposite law with greater force. You will then obtain a reversal effect. Have you ever watched two strong men arm wrestling? It is a picture of the law of reversal. When both men apply the same force, a holding pattern sets in; neither will give ground. However, as one man's arm is slowly pushed back towards its starting point, the greater power is seen. And this is exactly how the law of reversal works. So, if

> It is not enough to have the public language of enlargement and the private acceptance of barrenness.

the curse of barrenness is creeping into our lives and churches, it must be countered by applying an opposite law until it is broken and completely reversed.

The two great laws of the universe

There are basically two laws which compete for dominion in the universe. They are the 'Law of sin and death' and the 'Law of life in Christ' (Romans 8:2). The 'Law of sin and death' is found everywhere and it especially likes to operate in the church. Its driving force is Satan himself and its fuel is sin and rebellion against God - including our own when we walk in disobedience. The only way to break its power and reverse its effect is to apply the 'Law of life in Christ' with greater force until its arm is pushed back to where it came from.

Let me show you how this works. First, you must identify what particular law is the opposite of the one you want to reverse and start applying it. So, for instance, the opposite of 'lack' is 'plenty;' not 'just enough' or 'needs met' but 'plenty.' Some of you are stuck in a constant arm wrestling holding position; day in and day out you are battling to stay afloat

> You are only applying equal force when what you really need is some reverse thrust.

financially, emotionally and spiritually. That's because you are only applying equal force when what you really need is some reverse thrust.

The widow who cried out to Elisha for help was suffering under a severe lack attack. She was in huge debt and her creditors were coming to take her two boys as payment:

'The wife of a man from the company of prophets cried out to Elisha, "Your servant my husband is dead, and you know that he revered the Lord. But now his creditor is coming to take my two boys as his slaves." Elisha replied to her, "How can I help you? Tell me, what do you have in your house?" " Your servant has nothing at all" she said, "except a little oil." Elisha said, "Go around and ask all your neighbours for empty jars. Don't ask for just a few. Then go inside and shut the door behind you and your sons. Pour oil into the jars and as each is filled put it to one side." She left him and afterwards shut the door behind her and her sons. They brought the jars to her and she kept pouring. When all the jars were full she said, "Bring me another one." But he replied, "There is not a jar left." Then the oil stopped flowing. She went and told the man of God and he said, "Go and sell the oil and pay your debts. You and your sons can live on what is left."' (2 Kings 4:1-7)

Now watch this carefully. The first thing Elisha did was move the initiative from him to her. 'What do you have in your house?' In other words, where can we begin to reverse this curse of lack in your life? Where can we find an exit ramp from this road you are on? To Elisha the answer was simple; the exit from need is always seed. So, the question he asked was 'What have you got to start a reverse action

> **The exit from need is always seed.**

with? Most people who are in lack do the opposite and a siege mentality sets in. The last thing they think to do in lack is give anything away, so a withholding behaviour sets in. Holding on to what you have, cutting back, or trying to budget out what you've got to survive the crisis, will only create at best a parachute effect. It will slow down your fall but you are still going to hit the ground! What you need is some reverse thrust, which can only come from applying the opposite law with greater force. So, to give in a time of lack, and to keep on giving, allows the reverse thrust of plenty to begin to operate in your life. That reverse law can now attach itself to your generosity, whereas when you were withholding, it had nothing to attach itself to.

Here's how Jesus put it. He said: *'Love your enemies and pray for those who persecute you' (Matthew 5:4).* He said, if someone strikes you on the right cheek turn to him and offer him the other cheek also (Matthew 5:39). He said, if someone wants to take your tunic let him take your cloak as well (Matthew 5:40). He said, if someone forces you to go one mile, go with him two miles. In other words, go completely the other way and do the utter opposite of what is expected or required of you. By introducing the opposite counter-laws of love, peace and generosity, we push back the 'Law of sin and death' which is the force behind everything coming against us.

In Isaiah 54 God was revealing this principal to his people Israel and to us for today. Singing, bursting into song, shouting for joy and getting a bigger place, are all curse-reversing activities. Each of them released the opposite laws of breakthrough, productivity and enlargement to attach themselves to the corresponding actions. So, to do these things while still apparently barren is to release the opposite and desired effects into your life.

Go back for a moment to Paul and Silas in their prison cell. Through their action of singing at midnight in a nightmare situation, they triggered a curse-reversal effect into the atmosphere. Creation itself reacted at the precise point of reversal in the form of an earthquake. Clearly this was no natural earthquake. Phillipi is not in an earthquake zone and nowhere else was affected except the prison. What's more, the epicentre

> Through their action of singing at midnight in a nightmare situation, they triggered a curse-reversal effect into the atmosphere.

of the earthquake was above ground. This can never be true of a natural earthquake. The epicentre of this earthquake was the cell where two singing saints, Paul and Silas, refused to give in to the assault of the enemy on their call and vision, and thus allowed God to break in. The only damage done was that done to every instrument of bondage within the prison. Every door, bar, chain and lock was opened. It was as if the devil's wrestling arm was pushed so far back by Paul and Silas' singing, that a supernatural reversal took place in which the very atmosphere and state of the prison was transformed instantly into an 'open house.'

The Liberation of Creation

The earthquake at Calvary was another supernaturally caused earthquake (Matthew 27:51). The Cross was the greatest curse reversal ever initiated by God in the affairs of humanity. Calvary was the final reversal of the 'Law of sin and death.' At the point of shedding his blood, Christ said the three most

> The Cross was the greatest curse reversal ever initiated by God in the affairs of humanity.

powerful words ever uttered in human speech, 'It is finished!' Not 'I am finished.' He wasn't, what he came to do was finished. And when he said, 'It is finished!' the earth began to tremble under the weight of a completed work; under the weight of something no one else could ever have achieved for all generations. The spotless Lamb of God said just three words and then 'bowed His head.' It doesn't say, 'His head fell,' because he bowed it voluntarily, knowing a complete work was done. And the creation trembled in response.

Three days later, he rose from the dead! Do you know what he did then? He made a 'public show' of the enemy. That's the ridicule factor; God's big into ridiculing the enemy! (Colossian 2:15) God won't leave it alone. He made a public show of them; he rubbed the devil's nose in it! That's not an odd victory; that's not just

> Christ said 'It is finished!' Not 'I am finished.'

winning a race - that's triumph! That's complete and utter, over the top reversal. And it's time you had some in your life.

The Church: God's Reversal Agent

The Bible tells us that the whole of creation is waiting in anticipation for the manifestation of the sons of God; even creation itself cannot be liberated until the church of God live free and free indeed (Romans 8:18-23). And when we live free, we are going to see creation itself experience a reversal of the curse that's holding it in bondage.

You've never seen a tree until you have seen a tree that's been liberated from the curse! You've never seen a bird in flight until you see a bird in flight liberated from the curse! You've never seen a forest, a star or a sunset until you've seen them liberated from the curse of sin and their bondage to decay! All that we now see is tarnished and dull. But when the church rises up and becomes the people God intended us to be, creation itself will be liberated! The sun will shine brighter, the stars will be more beautiful than ever, the grass will be greener, the birds will sing more sweetly. Creation itself is waiting for you and me to explode into our fullness!

I believe that the church is God's curse reversal agent on the earth. Salt and light are reversal agents, they are not just withholding agents. They make a radical and immediate impact on their environment when they are introduced into a situation.

> The church is God's curse reversal agent on the earth

You are the 'salt of the earth' and you are the 'light of the world' (Matthew 5:13). We are a walking resistance movement against the curse of sin and death that seeks to assault our church, city and nation. We, the Church, are God's curse reversal agents.

CHAPTER FOUR

Incubation

Incubation

In this chapter I want us to explore the fact that verse two of our text in Isaiah 54 is all about the incubation stage of productivity. In it God does not say, 'Get a bigger tent' but 'enlarge the place' of the one you already have. This is a picture of a contained life, of cramped potential and stunted growth. Your tent is not too small, it's just contained.

Someone once said that the devil is 'Not half as concerned about pushing you back as he is about containing you where you are.' This is so true. The number of people in life who are functioning way below their potential is tragic. Sadly, they often make the mistake of thinking that they need a new life, a new start or a better opportunity. The 'if only' syndrome kicks in: 'If only' I had been born in that country, or at that time. 'If only' I had been given that opportunity. 'If only' I was like them, they don't have my disadvantages; they had a better education, a better childhood, a wealthy family - and so on.

> Your tent is not too small, it's just contained.

Your boundaries are inside you

'My son, attend unto my words;
Incline thine ear unto my sayings.
Let them not depart from thine eyes;
Keep them in the midst of thine heart.
For they are life unto those that find them,
And health to all their flesh.
Keep thy heart with all diligence;
For out of it are the issues of life.' (Proverbs 4:20-23 KJV)

The Hebrew word used here for 'issues' is literally the word 'boundaries.' So an alternative reading would be, 'Keep thy heart with all diligence, for out of it are the boundaries of life.' This means that the boundaries of your life are not determined by other people, or external circumstances, they are already in your heart. The boundaries of your life and the extent of your enlargement, is already within you.

The two main gateways to the heart are the eyes and the ears, what we see and hear. Because of what we have seen and heard throughout our lives, many of us are living inside false boundaries. Many false boundaries were established in childhood, boundaries of prejudice, fear, attitudes to authority, the opposite sex and money. These and many other potential boundaries were falsely erected in our hearts.

Only when people either come to Christ or become exposed to a different type of input, do they have any chance of discovering their true boundaries.

There is a definite, evil conspiracy to keep what God has placed in our hearts from coming out. Just imagine for a moment, how awful our world would be, if what was in some people's hearts had been prevented from coming out.

> The boundaries of your life are not determined by other people, or external circumstances, they are already in your heart.

Consider the effect on world architecture, transport systems and communication methods; the breakthroughs we have seen in medicine, the arts, business and music; the political reforms which resulted in the abolition of slavery, apartheid and communism. Millions of lives can literally be transformed by someone releasing what is in their heart.

That which is in your heart must 'come out' because it has to do with far more than you alone. The idea incubating in your heart could be an initiative that will bless and help thousands of lives long into the future. Many churches have stopped growing because the leadership has stopped living from their hearts. They have shut down that which is their 'issue of life,' because of resistance and persecution from controlling people in the church. The truth is that we may have to lose hundreds of people in order to gain thousands and we may have to lose thousands to gain millions.

A pastor asked me recently what was the biggest single key to the release and growth of our church. I didn't hesitate in answering that the biggest key was my own personal release and growth. Your life and ministry cannot grow beyond the boundaries of your heart. And I have learned that if your heart doesn't establish and then fight for its boundaries, you will live inside someone else's. That doesn't mean we all have to be in charge of everything, but we must all be in an empowering environment, one which draws out, encourages and makes room for what is in our heart to do.

A glimpse of God's ultra sound scan

When you have children, you soon learn that the conception was the easiest and shortest part of the process! The next stage, called pregnancy or incubation, is longer and one of incredible busyness. It is a time of preparation for that which is being incubated.

> Your life and ministry cannot grow beyond the boundaries of your heart.

We have four daughters, Charlotte, Bethan, Ruth and Esther. The middle two, Bethan and Ruth, are twins who are now 23 years old. I vividly remember the months of preparation that Glenda and I had to go through prior to the arrival of the twins. We had to enlarge the place of our own tent. For us that meant trying to find a bigger house that we could afford to rent. It meant me working overtime to enlarge our funds so we could afford to buy all the things we would need. Glenda had to enlarge her clothes size and appetite as her tummy stretched! Our relationships lengthened and stretched as we met other couples with twins. We purchased a twin buggy, two cots, two sets of clothing, multiple feeding bottles and sterilising formula. For months we bought boxes of disposable nappies to build up a stock in advance. We went to shops we didn't normally visit, watched programmes we wouldn't normally watch and had conversations with people we hardly knew.

All of this activity was based entirely on the evidence of a photograph called an ultra sound scan. This supposedly showed two babies but, being quite honest, they looked more like the dark side of the moon to me! However, those who knew how to interpret the ultra sound picture assured us that, without a shadow of a doubt, two babies were not going to arrive, but had already arrived.

'Enlarging the place of your tent' is therefore incubation activity because 'More shall be the children of the barren woman than of her who has a husband.' In other words, the song and the shout of the barren in verse one creates a conception moment, and the activity of verse two is the incubation period of preparation for the multiple birth God promised.

Have you seen God's ultra sound scan of your life and destiny? What preparations are you therefore making, during this incubation period, to get ready for the birth? Note I said 'birth' not 'arrival.' That's because it is already here in your heart, only the birth awaits. Maybe you need to get more education, learn another language or start saving some money. Whatever is required, start doing it now.

Preparation: The despised stage

Preparation is the most despised, and therefore the most neglected part of productivity. We love to start and we love to finish but we hate having to prepare for either. What's the worst part of decorating? You've got it - preparation! All that sanding down, scraping and filling. What's the worst part of going on holiday? Yes, you guessed it - packing! The worst part of a career are the years of preparation at school, college or university; especially all those exams! But unless you prepare, the birth will never be a success.

Here are some ways by which we can incubate something to its full term.

1. Confession:

Your confession is a verbal ultra sound scan. It shows what's incubating in your heart. Is your confession incubating your strengths or your weaknesses? Is your confession incubating your call, vision and ministry? Are your words fostering the development of your dreams and destiny? Our confession works both ways. By it we can also incubate problems, failure, lack, unbelief and fear. Whatever we are speaking about is what we are full of. Jesus said out of the overflow of the heart the mouth speaks (Matthew 12:34). When a woman is pregnant she talks all the time about the baby. In fact her whole world becomes shaped by the pregnancy. She discusses possible names, listens to other people's stories and talks avidly to other mums. Even though she had always wanted children and loved holding other people's babies prior to being pregnant, there is no comparison to the level of interest she now shows.

> Your confession is a verbal ultra sound scan. It shows what's incubating in your heart.

Have a confession check up, not when you are in a church meeting or surrounded by other believers, but when you are alone with just your own voice. Make sure that what you are believing for is what you are talking about, because like it or not, that's what you are going to receive.

2. Corresponding actions

A second way to incubate the dream in your heart is to do some corresponding actions. I have already mentioned all the things that Glenda and I had to do in preparation for the twin's arrival. However, it is absolutely amazing how many believers talk about what God has promised them but never seem to do anything about it. Wouldn't we consider it strange, to say the least, if we knew a couple were having a baby but they never spoke about it or did anything to prepare for it?

I regularly challenge my home church that if they believe God has called them to do something, they should start now preparing for that call. Don't say, 'I believe God is calling me to be a missionary to Spain,' but have no intention of learning to speak Spanish. Don't say, 'God has anointed me to be a

> All this talk without action is a 'phantom pregnancy;' it is all wind and no baby.

wealthy businessman and put millions into the kingdom,' if you don't tithe into the local church now. I have heard plenty of believers claiming to have an evangelistic calling but then never sharing their faith with their next door neighbour. All this talk without action is a 'phantom pregnancy;' it is all wind and no baby. And there are a lot of phantom pregnancies in the church today.

If some Christians put as much preparation into their destiny as their next summer vacation or new car purchase, then greater things would be happening throughout the world. You see, what is in you gains strength from the attention being paid to it. When the call, gift or vision you are incubating sees you preparing for its arrival, it grows and comes quicker. It's like planning to visit a friend overseas. In the months leading up to the visit you receive constant communication from them saying how much they are looking forward to your arrival and how many things they are planning for you to do together. The communication and the preparation guarantees a great visit. On the other hand, a lack of communication and preparation guarantees problems! I have sometimes arrived at a church to minister and felt like an interruption or an inconvenience to them. No one to meet me at the airport, no directions to the hotel, no information about

> What is in you gains strength from the attention being paid to it.

the meetings and no welcome whatsoever. One place draws you towards it with an eager anticipation, the other repels you away from it.

So it is with whatever we want to occur in our lives. We read in Hebrews 11:13

> What we welcome, comes towards us.

that many of the saints of old, knowing that they would never see the fulfilment of the promise of God to them in their lifetime, instead 'welcomed it from afar.' What we welcome, comes towards us. Whether we welcome it by thought, word or action, it will respond and travel in our direction.

I am incubating a church of thousands, so I am in constant thought, prayer and dialogue for that. What's in my heart is incubated by my confession and my corresponding actions. Let me explain:

*   When God spoke to me about going on television, I immediately began to incubate it into being by becoming TV minded, visiting TV stations, finding out what we needed to go on TV, investigating the costs and the technical side of programme production. One Sunday morning I placed three empty camera tripods, which I borrowed from a TV company, in the exact position where our cameras would go when we got them. Then in the meeting we called in the finances to buy those cameras; we called 'things that are not as though they

were.' Another thing we did was sow money into another TV ministry, naming the gift as seed for our own TV ministry. Within three months we were on air all across Europe and the rest is now history.

- When God spoke to me about starting a bus ministry, I immediately began to make enquires with people already running successful bus ministries. I flew six people out to Pastor Tommy Barnett's church in Phoenix, Arizona, to ride their buses for a week and get some in depth, behind the scenes practical experience. I also sent them with some financial seed to sow into Tommy's bus ministry. We have repeated this basic pattern of sowing to our harvest, time and time again, and it works every time without fail.

Are you expecting? If so, what are you expecting? Could I tell from your confession and actions what it is you are expecting without you telling me first? Could I tell from looking at your bedside reading material, or the tapes in your car, or the company you keep? All these things are the ultra sound scan of the inner miracle that you are incubating. It is time to enlarge your place!

> Could I tell from your confession and actions what it is you are expecting without you telling me first?

CHAPTER FIVE

Opportunity Aversion

Opportunity Aversion

'They're building your gallows'

Two years ago, only a few months before we broke ground on our new 2,000 seat church facility, I had an intimidating experience. One day as I drove into the car park I saw two men erecting a heavy wooden frame upon which they were about to mount a large sign which read: **'Future site of our new 2000 seater auditorium. Work starts Spring 1999.'**

In that moment, as I saw the sign going up and the heavy nails being hammered into the supporting frame, the devil spoke so clearly into my mind. He said, 'They are erecting your spiritual gallows and this project is going to hang you. It will fail financially, people will not support it and you will regret the day you ever started it. You will face national shame and humiliation when it all goes wrong. So stop now, quit while you can and stick with the building you have.'

Now you may think me very unspiritual and lacking in faith, but this assault from the enemy on my mind troubled me. For months, and well into the work being started, I never told anyone, not even Glenda my wife. Imagine my battle when half way through the project a group of about thirty people left our church because they didn't like the direction we were going in. They immediately stopped all their tithing and other giving, and withdrew their financial pledges to the building fund. The devil came back at me more strongly than ever, plaguing my mind by using this to prove his point.

I decided it was time for a serious word with God. If you've never had one of these, you don't know what you are missing! As I went to prayer, God immediately spoke and told me to re-read Isaiah 54. As I read this by now familiar scripture, I saw something I had never seen before, nor thought to be of any importance. The following words from verse two and four leapt off the page at me: *'Do not hold back... Do not be afraid, you will not suffer shame; Do not fear disgrace, you will not be humiliated.'*

God began to show me that I had a serious case of what I now call 'Opportunity Aversion.' Opportunity aversion works this way; when we come to the brink of an opportunity in life, especially if it's an opportunity that we have long waited and believed for, an attendant fear meets us at that point. The strategy of the enemy is to ensure that at the moment of our opportunity, we hold back because of the fear of failure and the intimidating thought of, 'What if this all goes wrong?'

I realised that every opportunity to succeed is also an opportunity to fail. If failure has been our more common, or recent experience, then our overwhelming tendency is to play it safe. There is shame and disgrace in barrenness, but there is also a fear of the potential shame and disgrace when we ponder breaking out and going for enlargement. Opportunity aversion is like an inner self-destruct mechanism that lies dormant until triggered by an opportunity. The opportunity of moving forward into greater freedom makes us feel vulnerable, so in the midst of the emerging freedom we feel the urge to cling to something familiar, which usually takes us back to the safety of our past. All too often, just as something is about to happen, just prior to our breakthrough, an aversion to proceed further seizes our mind and paralyses us from following through in obedience.

To a barren person, or church, future success is encapsulated in their simple desire to be free of barrenness. However, they need to realise that the breakthrough they want will also demand that they conquer doubt, fear and unbelief, sometimes on a daily basis.

> Opportunity aversion is like an inner self-destruct mechanism that lies dormant until triggered by an opportunity.

The apostle Paul described taking the opportunity this way: *'At the proper time we will reap a harvest if we do not give up, therefore as we have opportunity let us do good to all people'* (Galatians 6:9-10). I wonder how many 'God ideas' never happened because we 'gave up?' How many gifts and callings were never responded to and how many people remain unreached because of our opportunity aversion?

Not God's first choice

I remember Rienhard Bonke recounting the story of his first 'Minus to Plus' campaign here in the UK. When God asked him to do it he struggled at the enormity of the task. What settled it for him was that whilst in prayer one day, God told him, 'Rienhard you are not my first choice to do this, you are my third choice.' With the realisation that two other people had already said 'no' to God, he said 'yes.' Perhaps none of us are God's first choice for doing what we are doing. Maybe generations ago God asked someone else to do what you are now doing, but opportunity aversion frustrated God's purpose until you came along.

> I wonder how many 'God ideas' never happened because we 'gave up?'

Looking back two years to the event I described above, I now realise that the temptation to hold back was an 'enlargement staller.' Holding back was about to become a momentum breaker and once the momentum of my obedience had been

> Maybe generations ago God asked someone else to do what you are now doing, but opportunity aversion frustrated God's purpose until you came along.

broken, it would have been very difficult to recover. Many of you reading this book will not be responsible for major directional or financial decisions in your church, or the wider kingdom of God, but we all face opportunities in life and have to decide whether to take them or not. God's word to you is 'Stop holding back and go for it.' By all means get some wise advice and input but if it is clearly God, don't let the opportunity pass you by.

Shout for the ball

The Chicago Bulls are one of the best basketball teams in the world. They are probably more famous for having the great Michael Jordan on their team than anything else. One of my American friends who supports the Bulls, once told me that if in the closing minutes of the game the Bulls are losing, the most important thing at that point is to get the ball to Michael Jordan. They must get the ball to Jordan for two reasons: Firstly, he is the one most likely to sink it in the basket; and secondly, and more importantly, he is the only one that really wants it!

Many are envious of Jordan's wealth and popularity and many would die for the kind of sponsorship deals he has with companies like Nike. However these same people don't want the ball when it matters the most. When the

> 'Stop holding back and go for it.'

chips are down and there is only one point in it; when missing the last opportunity to score could be forever held against him, Jordan still shouts for the ball - and others on the team struggling with an Opportunity Aversion attack are happy to let him have it! The fame, fortune and popularity all go to the guy who shouts for the ball when no one else wants it. Whether he scores or not, the sheer courage he demonstrates inspires admiration from his fans which far outlive the game itself.

Do you want the ball? God is looking for people who want the ball in this generation. Shout for the ball of God's purpose for your church, city, town or nation. Shout out like Isaiah did in

> God is looking for people who want the ball in this generation.

the temple, *'Here am I, send me!'* *(Isaiah 6:8).* Stop playing deaf when God shouts your name. Don't be like Moses or Gideon who tried to talk God out of passing them the ball. Don't be found hiding in the baggage, like Saul, on the day of your opportunity. Instead, be like young David. Nobody was shouting for the ball when Goliath threw down his challenge to Israel's army except this young, rosy cheeked teenager. And for his courage he got the fame, the fortune, and the girl. They always do!

Who wants the ball in our generation?

From the dawn of time, God has been looking for people who are willing to carry the ball of his purpose into the world. After Adam fell, God found Noah and started again, repopulating the earth through him and his family. Following Noah, God found and called Abraham to carry the ball of his purpose. Then he found Isaac, Jacob and Joseph - and so on. In every generation God will find someone who really wants the ball and use that person to the full. He is not limited to church leaders, theologians, or so-called experts. God will use any willing person or thing, even animals. After all, in the past he has used a donkey, a whale, birds, frogs and locust's to mention but a few!

> In every generation God will find someone who really wants the ball and use that person to the full.

Many of the people God will find to run with the ball in our generation and the next, are not even saved yet. God is not limited to those who are currently born again. He is the God of all flesh not just 'the church', and his sphere of choice is humanity.

God's dot-to-dot

I have noticed that the people in this generation who are calling for the ball are finding each other; a global team of 'ball carriers' is emerging. I have discovered that in life and destiny, whoever you are looking for, is also looking for you. My friend Nancy Alcorn, of Mercy Ministries of America, describes it as God's great dot-to-dot puzzle, where all the dots have been positioned by God and then he sovereignly joins them up. When we were children joining up the dots of a puzzle, their position sometimes seemed to make no sense to us, we just could not work out what the picture was supposed to be. But eventually the whole, bigger picture began to emerge and it all made sense.

> God is putting together his own 'Dream Team.' He is gathering all the outstanding players from local club level, and sending them a call-up to play for the global Kingdom Team.

Don't be too quick to dismiss a connection that God is giving you. You never know how it will work, or how your 'dot' may become the key to releasing other 'dots' who are trying to find their place in God's greater purpose. These purpose driven relationships are key to breaking open towns, cities and nations for Christ. God is putting together his own 'Dream Team.' He is gathering all the outstanding players from local club level, and sending them a call-up to play for the global Kingdom Team. These 'best of the best' combinations are a formidable force and our world desperately needs them.

It is time to stop holding back. There is a 'ball' waiting to be carried across enemy lines and into a lost world. Shout for the ball of God's purpose today. Register your availability to God right where you are today. Don't let the fear of failure dominate you for another

> Today is the day to move from 'Opportunity Aversion' to 'Opportunity Attraction.'

moment. Today is the day to move from 'Opportunity Aversion' to 'Opportunity Attraction.' And you will be amazed at the opportunities that present themselves to you, as you resolutely decide to grasp them as they come.

CHAPTER SIX

Separation:
The First Act
of Possession

Separation: The First Act of Possession

We are now going to explore a principle that all believers must get to grips with if they are to fulfil their destiny. My heart is that you enjoy the enlargement and increase you desire for your life. And as you apply the principles I am sharing with you in this book, I am confident that you will never get stuck in the barrenness of Isaiah 54:1 but will live in the ever expanding enlargement described in verse 2. These timeless truths will empower you to spread out to the right and to the left, and to experience the joy of seeing your descendants dispossess nations!

> To possess the new thing God has for my life, I usually have to let go of something else which has become superfluous to the next stage of my journey.

To achieve this, we must first be willing to leave behind anything that has no place in our future. I have discovered that in order to possess the new thing God has for my life, I usually have to let go of something else which has become superfluous to the next stage of my journey. That 'something else' could be a person or a thing, an attitude or an action. It could be absolutely anything which is going to be excess baggage in my future. This principle is encapsulated in our chapter title, 'Separation: The First act of Possession.' Let me explain it to you from the life of Joshua.

The first thing that God said to Joshua was *'Moses my servant is dead'* (Joshua 1:2). Have you ever wondered why God would need to tell Joshua something so obvious? Joshua knew that Moses was dead, so this was not mere information. No, rather than information, it was separation. God was saying to Joshua, 'The life and times of Moses have ended; it is a new day of opportunity. So let's get this clear up front Joshua, Moses is dead, not sick, injured or coming back, but dead.' Though Moses' dream and vision of occupying Canaan was still very much alive, his ways, methods and style of leadership were not. Joshua had a massive job on his hands; he had to lead millions of people who had never known warfare into battle and then possess the land of Canaan. He had to move the people from a tribal mentality into nationhood. And all this was going to take place against a backdrop of incredible change in lifestyle and

> Joshua knew that Moses was dead, so this was not mere information... it was separation.

provision for the people. No longer would there be the cloud by day and the pillar of fire by night; no more breakfasts of Manna and dinners of quail conveniently provided each day.

> You can't enter your future and stay in your past.

From now on their provision would come from working the soil. It was therefore essential that, right at the outset of this new beginning, Joshua and the people both understood the significance of the statement, 'Moses is dead.' God was saying they couldn't have Canaan and keep Moses. And you can't enter your future and stay in your past. 'Moses is dead' was a final bridge-burning moment for Joshua.

'Moses' is the equivalent of anything or anyone that God wants you to move on from. It can be a person, an attitude, a mind-set, a method, a structure, place or position. Our Moses' will all be different, but we all have them. And God is saying to us, just like he said to Joshua, 'Moses is dead.' You see, what you cannot leave is where you stop. Sadly, many people have stopped in life because of attachments to people, places

> What you cannot leave is where you stop.

or things that God has said are dead. If you want to live a significant and productive life, you must always be willing to let go of whatever God has pronounced to be dead.

Separation was God's idea

God, not the devil, introduced separation. And he introduced it before The Fall of man showing that it was part of his perfect order. He separated day from night, animals from people, one species from another, male from female - and so on.

Separation for you and I began at birth when we were separated from our mother as the umbilical cord was cut. For new life to begin, an act of separation had to take place. Throughout life we then go through many other separations, some are gradual and involve no major decisions, whereas others are decisive turning points in life. Our transition from childhood to adulthood is gradual and occurs naturally over time, but sadly many adults remain childish by refusing to grow up and separate from what belongs to their childhood. The apostle Paul said: *'When I was a child I talked like a child, I thought like a child, I reasoned like a child. When I became a man I put childish ways behind me.'* (1 Corinthians 13:11) Paul would never have been used by God in the way he was, had he not understood the need to 'separate' in order to 'possess' his destiny and calling.

When our oldest daughter Charlotte got married I gave her away, not only to Steve her husband, but to a new life beyond her mother and I. This is just another form of separation introduced in the beginning by God. He said the man or woman must 'leave their father and mother' and be united to their marriage partner (Genesis 2:24). Separation is a natural and essential part of life.

Pruning is separation

Jesus said, 'I am the true vine and my father is the gardener. He cuts off every branch in me that bears no fruit, while every branch that does bear fruit he prunes so that it will be even more fruitful.' (John 15:1-2)

A gardener understands the necessity of pruning, the cutting back of fruitful, growing branches. The process of pruning is one of regularly removing the good in order to promote the growth of the best. To the untrained eye the cutting appears radical, ruthless and without thought. But to the gardener it's a joy, because like God, he prunes from a completion perspective. He knows that today's separation is tomorrow's increase. And so it is with our lives. Is

Today's separation is tomorrow's increase

God pruning something in your life, ministry or church at this time? Then greater growth and a higher yield are on their way. Don't fight God because the pruning knife seems to be moving towards your favourite roses. Believe me, they will be magnificent if they are pruned in God's season! God's knife has never slipped, he has never accidentally cut off something that should have remained on the plant, he is the perfect gardener. So relax and go with the flow of God's pruning knife in your life.

God is doing a 'new thing' which requires the separation of pruning to blossom into life. He says, *'Forget the former things, do not dwell on the past. See I am doing a new thing, now it springs up. Do you not perceive it?'* (Isaiah 43:18-19) Generally, our challenge lies not so much in embracing the future as it does in letting go of the past, especially if it has been a good

> It is easier to forget and move on from something bad than it is to move on from something good.

and blessed past. It is easier to forget and move on from something bad than it is to move on from something good. We simply cannot comprehend why God would want us to move on from someone or something that has been a blessing in our lives. So, we demand evidence that the person or thing is either wrong or bad before we become willing to separate from it. But as we have been saying, it is the good branches which are usually pruned!

If it's not broken, don't fix it

In the eyes of many a church congregation today, the pastor or leaders seem to be deliberately trying to upset them! They will insist on meddling with things that many in the congregation are happy with and feel should be left alone - they have an 'if it's not broken, don't fix it' mentality. But these men and women of God are, by gift and anointing, able to sense a spiritual 'settling down' in the church and are pruning things to promote the next wave of growth. They 'perceive it' wanting to 'spring up' and want to facilitate the 'new thing.' They are not tampering with things because they are necessarily bad or dysfunctional in the church, they simply sense the need to separate from some things to ensure the church remains in the vine and fruitful. Our challenge is to trust these God appointed and Holy Spirit anointed leaders, who are able to sense the winds of change. Then let's work with them to hoist our sails and catch this wind of change.

Moses is dead, but there's no body

'And Moses the servant of the Lord died there in Moab as the Lord had said. He buried him in Moab in the valley opposite Beth Peor, but to this day no one knows where his grave is. Moses was a 120 years old when he died, yet his eyes were not weak nor his strength gone.' (Deuteronomy 34:5-8)

A careful reading of this passage will help you understand why God had to emphasise to Joshua that 'Moses my servant is dead.' Moses was declared to be dead by God, and was buried by God, but no one saw him die. He wasn't sick, infact he was in great shape for a 120 year old! There was no body, no funeral and no grave. All the usual things we expect to have when someone dies were denied to Israel. They had no hard evidence that Moses was dead, nothing through which they could find closure and move on. Something very strange was going on here.

We gain further insight from the New Testament where we read about the dispute which took place over Moses' body. This was between Satan and the Archangel Michael (Jude 9). Why did the devil enter into a dispute with God about Moses' body? As far as we know this is the only one he ever disputed with God about, so it must be special. I believe that Satan was outraged at being denied the right of a body and a burial site for Moses' remains. He knew that if he could get a body and a gravesite, the vast majority of Israel would never move on. Moses was such an incredible figurehead, an icon, a man who spoke with God face to face. To them he was the greatest leader who had ever lived. Just imagine if there

> If he could get a body and a gravesite, the vast majority of Israel would never move on.

had been a gravesite, they would have turned it into a memorial shrine. It would have become a national monument from which they would have never moved on.

Knowing that this possibility was present, the devil seized upon the opportunity to put the nation 'on hold' and cause yet another generation to miss Canaan. He knew that their inability to separate from Moses would postpone their possession of the Promised Land. And you need to know that the devil will always settle for a postponement if he can't get a cancellation! The generation that gets postponed effectively cancel their own destiny. No, in these circumstances God could not allow there to be a gravesite. Canaan was ripe for the taking, he had a new leader in place and it was now or never.

Stop waiting for a body

Many of God's people are waiting for a corpse before they will accept that something God has finished with is dead. Because

> The devil will always settle for a postponement if he can't get a cancellation!

their 'Moses' who they must move on from isn't certified dead, they dispute with God about it. They would rather wait until that particular relationship or ministry gets sick and eventually dies. Then they can have a proper burial, some formal closure and eventually move on. But inevitably, by the time a thing is obviously past its 'sell-by date' or certified dead, all the problems associated with staying too long with something that God has finished with become evident.

Don't wait until a friendship goes bad before you adjust it and apply whatever degree of separation is necessary to either reinvent it, or leave it behind. Don't wait until a ministry, a meeting, a relationship or a church, are so far gone that you now feel justified in separating because it is obviously not working any more. Don't go looking for a corpse to prove that it's time to move on. Many of the things that God is telling you to separate from are, like Moses, still healthy, alive and walking around. The only closure you may ever get is God's word, which keeps telling you that your 'Moses is dead,' it is over, the season has come to an end, it's now time for you to move on to possess your promised future.

Separation releases your visitation

Abram was told by God to leave his country, people and father's household (Genesis 12:1). However,

> Don't go looking for a corpse to prove that it's time to move on.

we read that when he left, he took his young nephew Lot with him: *'So Abram left as the Lord had told him, and Lot went with him. Abram was 75 years old when he set out from Haran. He took his wife Sarai and his nephew Lot, all the possessions he had accumulated and the people they had acquired in Haran, and they set out for the land of Canaan and they arrived there.* (Genesis 12:4-5)

For some unknown reason, Abram compromised his obedience by taking Lot with him. His separation was not complete and he tried to take a relationship God said to leave behind into the future with him. It was not long before this compromise began to create problems for Abram:

> His separation was not complete and he tried to take a relationship God said to leave behind into the future.

'Now Lot, who was moving about with Abram, also had flocks and herds and tents. But the land could not support them while they stayed together, for their possessions were so great that they were not able to stay together. And quarreling arose between Abram's herdsmen and the herdsmen of Lot. The Canaanites and Perizzites were also living in the land at that time. So Abram said to Lot, "Let's not have any quarreling between you and me, or between your herdsmen and mine, for

we are brothers. Is not the whole land before you? Let's part company. If you go to the left, I'll go to the right; if you go to the right, I'll go to the left." Lot looked up and saw that the whole plain of the Jordan was well watered, like the garden of the LORD, like the land of Egypt, toward Zoar. (This was before the LORD destroyed Sodom and Gomorrah.)

So Lot chose for himself the whole plain of the Jordan and set out toward the east. The two men parted company: Abram lived in the land of Canaan, while Lot lived among the cities of the plain and pitched his tents near Sodom.' (Genesis 13:5-12)

What I want you to see is that because Abram stayed in a relationship after God told him to separate from it, major problems were caused by an ever-increasing circle of people. The longer we stay with something after God has 'called time' on it, the wider the circle grows of those who are damaged by it. Now this unhealthy relationship, which could have been left intact and on a high point back in Ur, is affecting families, employees and productivity.

Now see what happens to Abram after Lot has left:

'The LORD said to Abram after Lot had parted from him, "Lift up your eyes from where you are and look north and south, east and west. All the land that you see I will give to you and your offspring forever. I will make your offspring like the dust of the earth, so that if anyone could count the dust, then your

offspring could be counted. Go, walk through the length and breadth of the land, for I am giving it to you."'
(Genesis 13:14-17)

'The Lord said to Abram after Lot had parted from him...' There are some things that God is waiting to say to us. But he can't until we separate from our 'Lot' which interferes with our ability to hear clearly from him. Having eventually got Abram alone, God told him to lift up his eyes and said, 'All that you see is yours and your offspring's.' God re-centred Abram's life into his root calling. He had lost sight of the bigger picture by getting bogged down in the daily conflict with Lot, who had no business being there in the first place. Abraham's separation from Lot released a fresh visitation to his life, and although he still wasn't entirely free from Lot, he was separate enough to hear again the voice that first called him out from Ur of the Caldees.

> There are some things that God is waiting to say to us. But he can't until we separate from our 'Lot'

Annuals and perennials

In my garden I have two kinds of plants, annuals and perennials. The annuals last only a few months and then die because they cannot survive the winter. Perennials however, come back every year. They are hardy, able to survive the winter frosts and always burst into life again in spring.

So it is in our spiritual lives. God has designed some things to be annuals and some to be perennials. Some relationships, events, projects, roles and structures were never supposed to survive the winter. God's intention was for us to enjoy them while they lasted and then for us to allow them to die a natural death. So, if you are desperately trying to keep something alive that, left to itself would die, it is an annual and you should let it go. Perennials on the other hand, are things that God will ensure keep coming up again and again and need little or no effort from you to keep them alive.

Are you worn out trying to keep a friendship alive, trying to restore it to its former glory? Let it go, it was an annual. Are you staying up late and getting up early trying to make a ministry work? Let it die, it was an annual. I am not saying that we should not fight for a thing, or put in every effort to make something work. But there is a difference between appropriate effort and flogging a dead horse!

Why do we find it hard to accept that the eternal God will often use temporary forms of provision to help us? The truth is that most of the things we have made indispensable and deemed permanent, actually are not. In fact the apostle Paul who on numerous occasions went without food, shelter, protection, money, companionship or friends, boils everything down to just three enduring perennials: *'And now these three remain; faith, hope and love.' (1 Corinthians 13:30)*

From what, who, where and how do you need separation in your life? This separation is not the last thing that you must do, it's the first! Let go of what you cannot take with you, get free of any drag effect, become spiritually aerodynamic and remove all wind resistance. Throw your head back and run with all your heart for the 'tape' of your destiny.

> Separation is not the last thing that you must do, it's the first!

CHAPTER SEVEN

Iron Chariots

Iron Chariots

God's promise to the barren who will sing and prepare for increase, is not just to them but to their children and their children's children: *'For you will spread out to the right and to the left and your descendants will dispossess nations and settle in their desolate cities.'* (Isaiah 54:3)

Our potential increase is without limit as we continually apply all that we are learning about the laws of cause and effect, curse reversal and separation. God's intention for Israel was that she would be the 'head and not the tail, above and not beneath' (Deuteronomy 28:13). God intended his people to spread out in all directions, to influence every city and nation, and to bring his rule to every desolate and barren land. None of this has changed. In fact the need for the church to influence the world is more urgent than ever. We are the spiritual descendants of Abraham and it has now become our turn and our time, to advance God's kingdom in our generation.

Iron chariots

Under Joshua's leadership Israel successfully possessed and occupied much of the land of Canaan. The book of Judges then records the continuation of this period of history. Joshua was now dead and there were still many pockets of resistance and areas of land to be settled. So Israel set out to deal with all the remaining squatters and take full possession of their inheritance. Things went well and city after city fell before them. Israel seemed unstoppable, a dozen cities or more had fallen and the fear of them was upon all the land. Confidence, morale and faith were high. Then suddenly, in the midst of this growing momentum, the enemy produced something that stopped them in their tracks: ' *They took possession of the hill country but they were unable to drive the people from the plain because they had iron chariots.*' (Judges 1:19)

Chariots were common but not iron ones. They were usually made of wood protected by some metal plating but were still light enough to topple, crush or set fire to. But iron chariots were like modern day tanks, solid and strong, cutting a swathe through anything in their path. These iron chariots were a form of

> Iron chariots were a form of resistance never encountered before.

resistance never encountered before; they were an unknown quantity, without match in the Israelite arsenal. These military monsters said, 'So far and no further' to the Israelite advance. They broke both their spirit and momentum. And from here on everything went down hill. The run of conquests suddenly stopped and from this point on they never completely overcame and possessed another town or city.

Iron chariots in the church

Too often I have seen the strong and steady progress of a believer, or indeed an entire church, suddenly halted by a surprising form of resistance wheeled out by the enemy. These 'iron chariots' take many forms such as betrayal, sickness, bereavement, deception and sudden financial difficulty. The 'iron chariots' of abuse, infidelity, injustice and divorce can be absolute killers to once strong relationships. The world around us, which so needs God's kingdom life, is dominated by 'iron chariots' of prostitution, homosexuality, perversion, drugs, violence and organised crime. Throughout the world these forms of resistance exist as squatters in a land that God has given to us to enter and possess.

The devil fights dirty

Rumour, gossip and bad report are his stock in trade, and an unbridled tongue is his dream gift.

The devil fights dirty. He doesn't live by our rules. He has no conscience, no remorse and no mercy. He has come to 'steal, kill and destroy you' (John 10:10). And he will take any combination of these he can get. He will attack our families and friendships. He will assault our call, dreams and destinies. He preys on the weak and the vulnerable, and specialises in sowing discord between Christians. Rumour, gossip and bad report are his stock in trade, and an unbridled tongue is his dream gift. Sadly, many Christians are naively shocked by the low blows of the enemy but still live their lives so carelessly that he has many opportunities to do his worst.

The apostle Paul said, *'Do not give the devil a foothold'* *(Ephesians 4:27)*. A foothold starts at the threshold of our lives. If unchecked, the foothold becomes a stranglehold and finally a stronghold. Following this process, many 'iron chariot' problems can be found to have been invited into existence simply by our own carnality. They can therefore, just as easily be expelled by repentance and a return to a life of righteousness.

You need to know that there is no form of resistance that you cannot beat: *'No weapon formed against you can prosper'* *(Isaiah 54:17 KJV)*. You may, however, need to fight in a different way, fight with new allies or develop some new weaponry. God

> There is no form of resistance that you cannot beat.

knew all along about those iron chariots, they were not a surprise to him. So, if as you pursue God's call and an iron chariot appears to resist your progress, there is a solution. God knows how to beat iron chariots.

What we don't defeat our kids will have to beat

Several generations later in Israel's history, we read that the following advice was given to the king of Aram, one of Israel's enemies: *'Their gods are gods of the hills. That is why they were too strong for us. But if we fight them on the plains, surely we will be stronger than they.'* (1 Kings 20:23)

The failure of their forefathers to beat the first iron chariots created a legacy of defeat for their children and their children's children. Successive generations of Israel's enemies exploited this 'Achilles Heal;' Israel were weak on the plains. So time and time again they took the battle to the plain and defeated them there.

> Many of the 'iron chariots' we are now battling first appeared in our spiritual forefather's day.

Many of the 'iron chariots' we are now battling have been around a long time. They were forms of resistance that first appeared in our spiritual forefather's day. But instead of defeating them they cohabited with them. So what they didn't deal with in their generation, revisits us in ours, in an effort to intimidate us into settling for the same level of progress and achievement that they had. Generation in and generation out a pattern of containment begins to set in, where no major gains are made and maintenance of the old becomes all consuming. Our enemies gain strength and control over us, intimidating us through our repetitive weakness and our history of limited success. The fear of taking new opportunities and doing something no one else has ever done paralyses us, and yet again, opportunity aversion sets in.

Each generation feels a spiritual indebtedness to the one before it and, in some cases, are clearly dominated by the long shadow they cast into the present generation. The very idea of going beyond their achievements can be regarded as arrogant and presumptuous. If they couldn't beat a certain kind of iron chariot, who do we think we are? They could never plant a church in that town so what makes us think we can? They never went on TV so why should we? They never grew the church beyond a few hundred so why do we persist in talking about thousands? They were great men of faith but were never debt free, so what makes us think we can be debt free?

I believe that God intends every generation to go beyond the last one in faith, power, anointing, breakthrough, achievement and success. It is high time we beat some of the 'iron chariots' in our cities and nations. I do not want to hand my children a fight that was mine, or a problem that I was supposed to beat. I don't want them to start their race handicapped by things left undone and giants left unbeaten. I don't want things that terrorised me, to terrorise my children. I don't want people, systems or structures that dominated and contained me, to be passed on to them. Many democracy-ridden denominations are repeatedly handing a legacy of frustration to their spiritual children. Many legalistic and small-minded forms of church government are being allowed to scandalise our offspring, simply because we lack sufficient courage to change them, or fear the reprisals of the church Mafia if we even attempted to do so. Houses, salaries, cars and pensions can move from being expressions of love and support to forms of control, and the older we get the more we stand to lose by upsetting the status quo. An older pastor told me recently that although he was deeply troubled by the legalism and control of the church deacons, he was too near his retirement date to tackle it. I remember walking away with a heavy heart thinking about the young innocent about to be placed there from Bible College and the nightmare that awaited him.

> I do not want to hand my children a fight that was mine, or a problem that I was supposed to beat.

We should all want better for our children

Most parents want their children to do better than they did. We refuse to stand by and watch our kids go through the same disasters and heart aches that we went through. We do all we can to get them a better education than we had, better opportunities and better resources. We never think for one moment that our kids should go through the lack and hardship that we did, just so that they can earn it all the hard way.

When Glenda and I married, at the age of 16 and 17, we had absolutely nothing. Our first house was a back-to-back with stone flag floors containing just one room upstairs and one room downstairs. We had an old single tub washer and used a mangle to squeeze dry our clothes. Our toilet was outside, about 20 yards through an alley way and across a back yard. It was brick built with a gap under the door you could limbo under! We shared it with two other households. The house had no heating and was colder inside in winter than it was outside. It had mould on the walls and was infested with mice. Every piece of furniture in our humble home was donated to us, and we carried it up the street under the cover of night - after all we had some pride!

Now what parent in their right mind would want their kids to go through the same experience? My children were too young to remember that house and didn't believe there were such things as outside toilets. So, I had to take them back to our first house and show it to them. They fell about laughing in utter disbelief that anyone would put up with an outside toilet!

When Charlotte our oldest daughter married Steve, they moved into a lovely semi- detached home with all mod cons. They both had a car, good jobs and lots of nice things in their home. They bought much of their furniture new, had holidays abroad and ate out regularly. I can honestly say that Glenda and I never once let the thought cross our minds that they should have started their marriage in a house like we did. We were just so proud of them both and absolutely thrilled that they were off to such a strong start in their married life. As a parent I want my kids to do better than me, to have opportunities I never had and not have to wrestle with the same lack, shortage and hardship that we did.

Now why would I want this situation to be any different for my spiritual children? I intend to do all I can to clear the way for them to be able to achieve their maximum potential in their generation. Of course they will face their own challenges, which belong to them. But I will not stand idly by and watch someone oppress them who oppressed me, or things intimidate them that intimidated me. I will not allow anyone or anything to control and contain their anointing and destiny. I am prepared to stand my ground, state my case and fight my corner. I am prepared to be unpopular, spoken ill of, or even publicly maligned. I am prepared to stay up late, get up early, go any distance and drain my financial resources to protect my spiritual offspring. I am willing to lose people from the church and give up so called friendships for the sake of my spiritual children. I will live with being misunderstood, blamed for things I didn't do and crucified for things I did do. But I will never ever let an 'iron chariot' that was mine to defeat survive to threaten my children. I pray that, like old Caleb in his eighties, I too will say 'Give me this mountain. I am going to remove all the squatters on it and hand it to my sons and daughters debt free, conflict free and ready to be occupied.' May God grant us the courage to tackle our own 'iron chariots' of resistance and leave a legacy of freedom for the generations to come.

> But I will never ever let an 'iron chariot' that was mine to defeat survive to threaten my children.

The resurrection: The ultimate legacy of victory

Through the cross, resurrection and ascension, Jesus secured an eternal victory over the devil. The apostle Paul tells us that: *'Having disarmed the powers and authorities he made a public spectacle of them, triumphing over them by the cross.'* (Colossians 2:15)

This was a once-for-all-time triumph. This was the ultimate follow through to ensure a complete and unequivocal victory for the generations of the church to come. This is still our ground of victory. We don't need to fight the devil all over again in every generation; Jesus beat the devil once and for all! We stand in the completed work of Calvary. The war has already been won. Jesus, our Joshua, has taken the land. What we are

> The war has already been won. Jesus, our Joshua, has taken the land.

now experiencing are a few remaining skirmishes with the remaining principalities and powers, who still attempt to postpone the inevitability of their eternal consignment to hell.

Jesus did such a complete work that there remains no form of resistance that we cannot overcome - not one. So, the next time the devil wheels out an 'iron chariot' to resist your progress, remember that it's only fuel is your fear, and that it has already been beaten for you through the cross, resurrection and ascension of your Lord Jesus Christ. So, iron chariots - let them come!

CHAPTER EIGHT

Multiplication

Multiplication

Multiplication is accelerated addition. Multiplication is having it sooner, arriving faster, leaping higher and understanding more quickly. Multiplication by-passes waiting, it is 'all at once' and 'suddenly.' Multiplication is learning in a week what it took our forefathers five years to learn. It is achieving in a day what previously took many years to accomplish. It is birth without labour, delivery without pain and a nation brought forth in a moment, as Isaiah prophesied:

'Before she goes into labour she gives birth; before the pain comes upon her she delivers. Who has ever heard of such a thing? Who has ever seen such things? Can a country be born in a day or a nation be brought forth in a moment? Yet no sooner is Zion in labour than she gives birth to her children.'
(Isaiah 66:7-8)

The church knows all about addition and duplication. She also knows a great deal about division and subtraction. But I believe it is time we saw some multiplication in and through the people of God.

The X factor

The mathematical sign for multiplication is X. This tells us how many times the original number is to be multiplied by. So for instance 3 x 5 = 15. I know this isn't exactly rocket science, but stay with me! I want to show you something very exciting. In maths the outcome of a multiplication sum is predictable because the value of the numbers are already known. So, 3 x 5 will always be 15. However, God has promised to be the multiplication factor in our increase and enlargement, so he becomes our

> And if we are multiplying by God, how many are we multiplying by?

X factor. Therefore instead of 'x5' it becomes 'xGod'! And if we are multiplying by God, how many are we multiplying by?

In Isaiah 54, God's promise to barren people who will sing and shout for joy, and get ready for increase, is multiplication by another name: *'More shall be the children of the desolate woman than of her who has a husband.'* (Isaiah 54:1) In other words, one woman's X factor is her husband but yours is going to be God himself! Natural multiplication is one thing but the outcome of multiplying by God is unpredictable and uncommon. I don't know about you, but I wouldn't mind some uncommon and unpredictable multiplication in my personal, church and ministry life! When God is the number by which

One woman's X factor is her husband but yours is going to be God himself!

our lives are being multiplied, nothing is predictable, outcomes are unknown, the normal and ordinary can no longer dominate, and new things become possible.

Our past is not our future. The benchmark of what can be achieved in our generation is not history but our present faith. If history is the governing factor for today's achievements, as some pessimistically forecast, God is a prisoner of history - and that cannot be.

Jesus' first multiplication miracle

Jesus' first recorded miracle was turning water into wine at a wedding in Canna, Galilee:

'On the third day a wedding took place at Cana in Galilee. Jesus' mother was there, and Jesus and his disciples had also been invited to the wedding. When the wine was gone, Jesus' mother said to him, "They have no more wine." "Dear woman, why do you involve me?" Jesus replied. "My time has not yet come." His mother said to the servants, "Do whatever he tells you." Nearby stood six stone water jars, the kind used by the Jews for ceremonial washing, each holding from twenty to thirty gallons. Jesus said to the servants, "Fill the jars with

water"; so they filled them to the brim. Then he told them, "Now draw some out and take it to the master of the banquet." They did so, and the master of the banquet tasted the water that had been turned into wine. He did not realize where it had come from, though the servants who had drawn the water knew. Then he called the bridegroom aside and said, "Everyone brings out the choice wine first and then the cheaper wine after the guests have had too much to drink; but you have saved the best till now." This, the first of his miraculous signs, Jesus performed at Cana in Galilee. He thus revealed his glory, and his disciples put their faith in him.' (John 2:1-11)

Turning water into wine was a miracle of multiplication. Instead of waiting for the usual fermentation process to take months to change the water to wine, Jesus did it in an instant by changing the x factor from nature to himself. He simply by-passed the waiting time and reduced the whole process down into a matter of seconds. Now here is the best part. When it was served to the master of the banquet he couldn't believe the quality and declared it to be the best wine he had ever tasted. You see when God multiplies something, quality is retained. That is

> When God multiplies something, quality is retained.

because God does not rely on time or natural processes to achieve quality. Don't listen to those doom and gloom merchants who criticise your success by implying that you must have compromised or taken a short cut on quality to get there. God never compromises on quality.

Pace and process

Multiplication brings acceleration to two primary areas, they are pace and process. When you accelerate in your car on the motorway both your pace and process change immediately. You are simultaneously moving faster (pace) and rearranging your position in relation to the other vehicles (process). The speed of your journey is being multiplied by the acceleration you are willing to generate with your right foot. If you travel inside the speed limit, then the time of your journey and estimated time of arrival are easier to calculate. If however, you drive faster than the speed limit, you seize control of your pace from the external restriction of the Highway Regulations and transfer it to your personal choice. Now I'm not advocating that we all break the law and start speeding, I am simply illustrating the point!

So for example, when visiting the USA where the speed limits are so low, I may ask a friend how long it will take to drive between two certain points. They answer me from a national speed limit point of view - which makes every journey sound like it will take forever. However that's not how I listen, I listen from a 5 litre Lincoln Town Car point of view! In my mind the time of my journey is not governed by the external speed limit but by the internal power of my engine. Now here's my point, who sets the limits for the speed of your spiritual life? Is it the recommended speed of the 'play it safe' crowd? Is it the recommended speed of the legalistic 'I have never broken a law in my life' crowd? Is it simply

> We all have far more power under the bonnet than we are using and most of our vehicles are under performing.

what has become the norm around you because that's how everybody drives? Is it the corporate speed limit of your church, group or movement? The fact is that we all have far more power under the bonnet than we are using and most of our vehicles are under performing.

Many years ago I used to drive a 3-tonne Box Van to deliver carpets. The accelerator pedal on that vehicle had a metal stud attached to its underside to act as what is called a 'governor.' When you pressed the accelerator pedal down, the vehicle wouldn't go any faster because the metal stud was stopping it. So, I would secretly remove the metal stud, not just because I wanted to drive faster, but because I just could not stand having my personal choice removed by a governor. I have always been a bit of a rebel! But then again, I have always seemed to get things done quicker than others.

Are there governors in your life? If so, what or who are they, and what are you going to do about it? The speed limit of your growth, call and destiny must never be surrendered to controlling smaller people, who are not trying to get where you are going. Nor must you ever stop to pick up a hitchhiker who requires you to take a detour to drop them off somewhere else. That is hijacking, not hitchhiking, and it has no place in your life.

Road rage

Road rage is a terrible thing. Normal, peaceful, and apparently sane people, turn into lunatics in seconds because someone overtakes them, takes a parking space they wanted or cuts them off in traffic. I have seen mothers with children in the car wind down the window and shout abuse at other drivers. I have seen old gentlemen shake their fists and respectable looking businessmen use hand gestures that do not appear in the Highway Code! We stare in disbelief at this Jekyll and Hyde behaviour, but I've got news for you it is nothing compared to the spiritual road rage I have witnessed in the church.

> The speed limit of your growth, call and destiny must never be surrendered

Here's the other side, the down side of multiplication that no one talks about. If you overtake someone spiritually, or move into a ministry they wanted, or drive too fast for their liking, they can get a serious case of spiritual road rage. You see everybody wants multiplication and multiplication, as we have already seen, brings an acceleration which immediately affects pace and process. But touching these things makes some

> **If you overtake someone spiritually they can get a serious case of spiritual road rage.**

people angry! If you want to find out who the 'control freaks' are in your church, just touch pace or process. You will soon hear from them.

Pace and process are the two most essential elements within any organisation. Whoever controls the pace and the process controls everything. The speed with which things happen and the way in which things happen are usually the exclusive and protected domain of a few at the top. People can make as many recommendations or express as many ideas for change as they like, but nothing will change until those who control the pace of response and the process of change decide to get moving.

Fast forward

Nothing stays the same when God's divine acceleration kicks in. Everything goes into fast forward. Just like when you watch a video in fast forward mode, everything that happens in the movie is still happening but it is happening so fast it cannot be properly identified or explained. The prophet Amos put it this way:

'The days are coming,' declares the LORD, 'when the reaper will be overtaken by the ploughman and the planter by the one treading grapes.' (Amos 9:13)

This is a classic multiplication scripture. It depicts exactly what happens when pace and process are speeded up. People and roles that would normally follow one another begin overtaking each other. The ploughman who is normally at the beginning of the process overtakes the reaper who is normally at the end of the process. The grape treader who is usually separated by months of

> **Many want multiplication and divine acceleration but not if it means us being over taken by someone who has normally followed us.**

process before his role is required, suddenly overtakes the planter who is normally the earliest stages of the process.

Many want multiplication and divine acceleration but not if it means us being over taken by someone who has normally followed us. When Jesus turned water into wine all the wedding guests were blessed. But the winemaking industry would not have been happy if it thought this was going to be a regular occurrence!

What does all this look like in practice? It means that people who have taken two years to plant a new ministry will suddenly be over taken by some 'Johnny come lately' who is already drinking the new wine of his new initiative which seemed to spring up overnight in comparison. It means that those who are tending a carefully nurtured Sunday School programme, will be overtaken as God ploughs it all up by using people with new ideas and initiatives, which bring in thousands of kids that the old-style Sunday school would never have reached. Behold I show you road rage! You haven't seen carnality until things that used to follow people start overtaking them, and those who were in control are suddenly discharged, not by men, but by God's divine acceleration.

God is taking the brakes off. He is removing the governors and ignoring our traditional speed limits. He couldn't care less what we think about his driving or his choice of co-drivers. He will not slow down, turn around or be hijacked. There is a world to be reached and he is going for it, with or without us.

He who pays the piper

This well known phrase originated in Scotland, where people would gather around in the Taverns or at social events and ask the piper to play their favourite tune. However, the piper would only play the tune of the person who first paid him. Hence the phrase, 'He who pays the piper calls the tune.'

Both Jesus and John the Baptist were expected to 'dance to the tune' of either Rome or the religion of their day. Jesus put it this way as he responded to the various 'tune-requesting' voices of his day:

'To what can I compare this generation? They are like children sitting in the marketplaces and calling out to others: "We played the flute for you, and you did not dance; we sang a dirge, and you did not mourn." For John came neither eating nor drinking, and they say, "He has a demon." The Son of Man came eating and drinking, and they say, "Here is a glutton and a drunkard, a friend of tax collectors and sinners." But wisdom is proved right by her actions.' (Matthew 11:16-19)

The JB Philips New Testament puts it this way: *'We piped to you playing wedding songs but you wouldn't dance; we played funeral dirges but you wouldn't cry.'*

Whose tune are you dancing to? To whom or to what have you

obligated yourself by promising to dance to their tune? It could be a controlling person, a dominating boss, a controlling habit, the dictates of your history or legalistic church members. Are you dancing to the 'I'm only a single parent' tune? Or maybe the 'I'm a divorced person' tune? Or even the 'I'm an ethnic minority' tune? These are the tunes of your circumstances. Don't let them define your life, circumstances are simply the circle in which you stand, they are not your life, value, ability or status. Be like Jesus, refuse to dance to any other tune except that of God's will and purpose for your life.

> Circumstances are simply the circle in which you stand, they are not your life, value, ability or status.

Over the years I have been pressured to dance to the various tunes played by controlling people in the church. But I would rather tango with God, than slow-waltz with the devil or hokey-cokey with flaky Christians! Over recent years, the more I've refused to respond to a lesser tune, the more God has blessed our church, and the more we have attracted a different kind of people - people all dancing to the same tune of God's purpose for our church and ministry. They say that 'Birds of a feather flock together,' and people hearing the same heavenly tune do too!

Multiplication means giving up control

For the past three years now, I have had the distinct feeling that I am no longer in control of my home church. I don't know everything that's happening or some of the people making it happen. I wasn't part of the decision-making teams which birthed and launched some of our new ministries. I no longer know who many of the people are who sing in the choir, serve in kids church or play in the band. And I can honestly say it has been the best thing that ever happened to both our church and me. I am not talking about abdication or irresponsibility but rather the difference an empowering culture can make. It is as if God had been waiting for years for me to relinquish control and empower people to live their dreams. Multiplication makes things happen so fast that trying to control and contain everything is useless. Sadly, many leaders cannot live with relinquishing control; it goes against both their natural instincts and formal training. But you need to know that multiplication will mean giving up control once and for all. I have had to learn this, both in my own house and in God's house. The truth is that whatever I cannot let go of, I don't really have anyway, it has me.

> God had been waiting for years for me to relinquish control and empower people to live their dreams.

I pray God's multiplication on you, your church and your ministry. May you know the joy of being overtaken by things that are travelling in the same direction as you. After all, it doesn't really matter what the respective

> **Whatever I cannot let go of, I don't really have anyway, it has me.**

positions of the planter, reaper, ploughman or grape-treader are. What matters, is that they are all making wine! And remember, the shorter the time lag between discovering a person's ability to serve and putting that into an actual ministry, the more effective you will be.

CHAPTER NINE

God's New Wineskin

God's New Wineskin

There was once a woman who owned the finest winery in all the land. Everything about it was superb. The fertile land yielded some of the finest grapes to be found. The large wooden vats, that nurtured the crushed grapes until maturity, produced the world's most exquisite wine. For more than two centuries people came from all over the world to visit the winery and drink the famous wine.

One day the wine developed a bitter taste. No one could explain why. Nothing had changed. The wine was still made exactly as it had been for the last two centuries. Visitors and customers began to decline. In desperation the woman hired consultants from all over the world to discover the reason for the wine's sudden bitter taste. After days of study each expert arrived at the same diagnosis, the vats had outlived their usefulness. They were old and sour with no way of been cleaned and restored. The consultants concluded that her only option was to replace the old vats.

She was outraged. The beautiful vats had been in her family longer than she had and were not about to be replaced. So, she made desperate attempts to improve the wine. She added new fertilisers to the ground which changed its acidity, designed new labels for the bottles, and even hired a new overseer for the vineyard. But she continued to put the wine into the old vats. And the finest grapes in the world continued to produce bitter wine. To the woman, family traditions were more important than the decline of her winery.

The number of visitors and customers continued to diminish until the day arrived when no one came to taste or buy the wine. The only remaining customers were the faithful members of the family, for whom family traditions were more important than making satisfying wine.

The owner of the winery knew why the grapes were making bitter wine. She had all the knowledge she needed to restore her winery to its former glory. But she lacked the courage to use the knowledge at her disposal. Family traditions ran too deep to replace the precious vats. In time, the

> Family traditions were more important than the decline of her winery.

world famous vineyards fell into ruin and only family members continued to drink the bitter wine. Jesus said:

'No one sews a patch of un-shrunk cloth on an old garment, for the patch will pull away from the garment making the tear worse. Neither do men pour new wine into old wineskins. If

they do the skins will burst, the wine run out and the wineskins be ruined. No, they pour new wine into new wine skins and both are preserved.' (Matthew 9:16-17)

God is doing a new thing! He is not doing a new thing within an old thing, or as well as an old thing, or in competition with the old thing; he is just doing a new, fresh, relevant thing made for our time. Sadly, much of the church and her leadership are wedded to an old thing. Religion has replaced relationship and religion is what's left after God has gone.

Like the woman in the story who owned the once great winery, the religious leaders of Jesus' day were unwilling to embrace the new, and for them tradition was more important than relevance. In addressing them, Jesus basically said you can't use the new to patch up the old and you can't use the old to contain the new. To us today he may have said you can't replace the old church organ with an electric keyboard and call it God's new thing. You can't take off your clerical collar and hang up your clerical robes, put on leather pants and call it God's new thing. Renaming House Groups as Cell Groups and attending a Cell Church conference won't do it either.

Some churches are like a patchwork quilt with bits from everywhere. A patch of contemporary worship, a piece of Toronto blessing, some Pensacola sown in, a bit of faith teaching here and a hint of prosperity teaching there. And finally a little dash of Ephesians four ministries to keep that crowd happy. The problem is that all these pieces of new cloth are stitched onto the underlying old garment. They are little more than a veneer, a camouflage, for that which has no intention of changing.

All this activity is like rearranging the deck chairs on the Titanic - no matter what you do, unless you change course you are going down. History records that the captain of the Titanic had six warnings to change course but refused to do so because he believed his ship was unsinkable. He also wanted to prove that his ship could cross the Atlantic in record time. We all know what happened, an iceberg sliced open the ship's hull and within a few hours fifteen hundred people had drowned.

If we do not change the course that we are on, the fate of much of today's church will be no different. Unless the ship is taken off autopilot and the numerous warnings heeded, icebergs with names on are waiting to sink so-called unsinkable churches and ministries. It is one thing to be hit by an unforeseen problem, it is another when the thing that sinks us was known to us all too well. Icebergs called, 'irrelevant,' 'the status quo,' 'our comfort zone,' 'dead traditions,'

> Icebergs with names on are waiting to sink so-called unsinkable churches and ministries.

'control,' 'democracy' and 'pride,' are all waiting to sink us if we do not change course.

Madonna has more sense than most church leaders

The pop star Madonna just keeps on going from success to success. She has realised that if she does not continually reinvent herself, her career could have been well over by now. The singer Tom Jones is another good example. He is now teaming up with some of the young, chart topping bands and doing new songs, albums, TV appearances and tours with them. 'Has beens' are people who refused to change direction whilst arrogantly believing that they were unsinkable. Whatever you do, don't become a 'has been!'

Everything that is prospering does so because it is willing to change, whether in business, politics, medicine, entertainment or sport. Why then is it that many people in the church, who work all week in a fast changing Hi-Tec environment, resent and resist change in the church? Maybe they see the church as an oasis of stability and familiarity in a changing world. They crave sameness, tradition and predictability. Even though they are bored to tears by the church service, their security is anchored in ancient rituals and observances that have remained unchanged for generations. In fact, many people's attendance, serving and financial giving is actually conditional upon the leadership leaving some of these things alone. And just to make sure nothing changes, they surround and neutralise the leadership with controlling committees, boards of trustees and deacons. I have been to enough 'deacon-possessed' churches to know that it is easier to drive demons out of possessed people than it is to drive out the controlling deacons!

The life is in the new

When Jesus spoke about patching a piece of cloth, he was teaching a spiritual truth using an every day example. An old garment will be torn if a patch of new cloth is attached to it, because the new cloth hasn't stopped moving yet. New cloth is prone to movement by stretching or shrinkage. It is still flexible, responsive and reactive if exposed to certain elements. An old garment however, has stopped moving; the life has been washed and

> If you attach something that is moving to something that has stopped, tearing and separation is inevitable.

worn out of its fibres. Jesus was simply saying that if you attach something that is moving to something that has stopped, tearing and separation is inevitable.

It is like spiritual bungee jumping. Eventually the jumper's free-fall is broken by the reverse force of the elastic rope which is attached to something that will not move. Have you just jumped into God's new thing? Well everything and everyone that has stopped moving in your life, church or ministry is about to yank you back! Some of you reading this may already have spiritual whip lash, while others are still in free-fall - you haven't gone far enough to discover you are attached to something that has stopped moving.

The same thing happens when new wine is stored in an old wineskin. The movement in the new wine fractures the old skin which has become rigid with age. The inflexible wineskin lacks sufficient life in itself to accommodate and move with the vibrant new wine. Tearing and spillage is inevitable.

Why is it that those involved in the last move of God always seems to be the most resistant to the next? Jesus was persecuted by the Pharisees of his day, a devout God-fearing people who had once walked with God and been key players in doing a new thing at a crucial time in Israel's history. Martin Luther was persecuted by the Catholic Church, John Wesley by the Anglican Church, and William Booth's Salvation Army was frowned on by all of these. This is the pattern of Church History. Sometimes the lines of conflict have been obvious and at other times they have been more subtle. Whichever, the old always seems to have a tendency to undermine and resist

God's new thing. Our challenge is to break that pattern.

How do I know I am stopping?

There are two primary things to look for. Firstly, if you are somewhat bewildered and asking the question, 'What is happening to our church?' It is a sure sign that you are stopping. Only people who are not making something happen, ask what's happening. It is the same in all areas of life. For example, if you say 'What is happening to my marriage?' Then whatever is happening is not coming from you! Similarly with your money. To admit that 'I just don't know what is happening to my finances' means that whatever is happening, is happening through some other influence. It is only a spectator who asks the question 'What is happening?' And if you are spectating your own life, job, church or family you have simply stopped making it happen.

> Only people who are not making something happen ask 'What's happening?'

> You are stopping if everything else moving around you deepens your sense of isolation.

Secondly, you are stopping if everything else moving around you deepens your sense of isolation. Have you ever broken down in your car by the side of the motorway? If so, you will no doubt recall that the time sat waiting for the road side assistance to arrive seemed like an age. Your immobility was reinforced by every passing vehicle. Everything that's still moving deepens your sense of frustration that you're not going anywhere. O how we would love it, if everyone would just stop and wait with us rather than zooming past at what seems like 200 miles per hour from our stationery perspective. But all we get are the back drafts from their vehicles as they whiz by. Everything that is moving reinforces the fact that you are not, and often by the time the breakdown services do arrive we are therefore in no mood for pleasantries!

Have you ever been stranded in an airport due to a delayed flight? While you sit going nowhere, surrounded by everyone else going somewhere, your frustration mounts. Every plane that takes off reinforces the fact that you are not moving. It is the same in the church. Everyone that is moving forward and going for God

> Resist the temptation to fight against what is moving, and instead find out why you have stopped.

will reinforce your sense of isolation if you have stopped. The challenge is to resist the temptation to fight against or sabotage what is moving, and instead find out why you have stopped. Get some 'breakdown assistance' and get back on the road!

If you are asking 'What is happening?' or are upset by what is moving around you, then you have either stopped or are stopping.

Why the dinosaurs became extinct

In his book 'Dancing With Dinosaurs,' William Easum states: 'No one knows scientifically why dinosaurs became extinct. Perhaps over time the plant growth was stunted and stopped growing so high due to the dinosaur's tremendous appetite... Still, food was plentiful if the dinosaur merely bent down to reach the lower vegetation. But perhaps the dinosaur's neck was too stiff to bend down to the vegetation. Or maybe the dinosaur was too short sighted to see the lower vegetation. Perhaps the dinosaurs became extinct because of their unwillingness or inability to see what was happening all around them... Congregations, whose membership has plateaued or who are in decline, have much in common with dinosaurs. Both have great heritages. Both require

> Faced with a radically changing world many are unwilling to feed where they have never fed before.

enormous amounts of food. Both influenced their world tremendously. And both became endangered species. Will many of today's churches, like the dinosaurs, become extinct?

Many churches today show all the signs of the same problem. Like the dinosaur they have a voracious appetite. Much of their time, energy and money is spent foraging for food, so that little time is left to feed the unchurched. And faced with a radically changing world many are unwilling to feed where they have never fed before. Either their pride or short-sightedness keeps them from changing the ways they minister to people.'

Don't let your life, ministry or church become a dinosaur. Be determined to go anywhere, talk to anyone, read any book, sit under any ministry or serve anyone necessary, to make sure that you stay relevant, productive and full of life.

Martha

I have found the following story about the extinction of the passenger pigeon very instructive.

The last remaining passenger pigeon in existence, an old female called Martha, died in captivity at Cincinnati Zoo in 1914. One hundred years earlier, a single flock of these birds could number over 2 billion and there were multiple flocks throughout Eastern America. In 1813 a man named John Audubon observed a migrating flock over Kentucky. He reported that the sky was black with birds for three days, their nesting colonies could be 20 miles across with so many birds per tree that the branches broke under their weight. There isn't a single passenger pigeon left for us to observe today.

Now read this next point carefully! One theory explaining the passenger pigeon's inability to recover is that their breeding pattern required a community of many other breeding pairs in order to stimulate the necessary cycles. As numbers declined, the scattered distribution of the remaining birds thus made it very difficult to find suitable mates.

The church alive is worth the drive

You may have to search far and wide to find a suitable spiritual mate to help you conceive and incubate what is in your heart. But that's better than extinction. You may have to get on a plane, surf the Internet or drive to another part of your country. In my home church we have people driving one and a half hours each way to get to our Sunday services. This is very unusual for England. But people are finding out that a church alive is worth the drive.

To my shame, for the greater part of the first twenty two years of my Christian life, I rarely attended a conference, meeting or seminar outside the tight-knit network of churches I belonged to. I rarely listened to tapes or read books by authors outside of my group. I didn't have anyone minister to the church that wasn't either sent or approved by those over me. A few years ago when I became separate from that network, I began searching for new spiritual input, fellowship and relationships to help me personally and our wider ministry. I was determined not to become like that last

> I was determined not to become like that last remaining carrier pigeon called Martha.

remaining carrier pigeon called Martha. As I searched, I found enough like-minded species to draw from and together we began a brand new colony of 21st century carriers for God. To my delight I found these fellow pilgrims in four places:

1. Around me in my own church
2. Within driving distance in the UK
3. In countries all across the world
4. In books and tapes

And I am still looking for more!

If you are also looking for your purpose driven relationships, then here is a clue about where to look. Look to the outer limits of what normally passes for being generally acceptable. The future is at the fringe, on the cutting edge, somewhere near the outer limit of religious respectability. There, God is pioneering his new thing. Every one of my current staff of twenty are people like that! The oldest is 44 and the youngest 22. The majority are in their 20's. Though it is not necessarily about age, I have found that this kind of people have little or no church baggage, have tons of life, are very flexible, willing to take risks and are a little bit crazy! Most of the disciples were teenagers when Jesus called them, so be encouraged.

> The future is at the fringe, on the cutting edge, somewhere near the outer limit of religious respectability. There, God is pioneering his new thing

In closing, here are a few of the ways in which we as a church have reinvented ourselves over the last three years. These few words each describe an emphasis we have consciously moved on from and something of what we have now become:

We have moved from

People centred
Controlling
Tradition driven
Structure led
Making our feet fit the shoes

Professional pastoral care
Holding evangelistic events
Come to us
Keeping the aquarium

To become

God centred
People empowering
Purpose driven
Vision and life led
Making shoes that fit our feet

Mutual care for one another
Soul wining culture
Go to them
Catching fish

I hope this book has been a blessing to you. My prayer is that you will now use the tools provided in these pages. They will equip you to break, and stay away from barrenness; they will help you to shape a new future, one filled with productive activity for God and the thrill of spiritual adventure. Just always remember, no matter what is going on in your life right now, or how bad things may appear to be, **It's not over 'til the barren woman sings!**

Also by the same author:

God's Fingerprint

You can obtain further details about Abundant Life Ministries and a copy of our free magazine 'A Voice to the Nations' from:

Abundant Life Ministries
Abundant Life Centre
Wapping Road
Bradford BD3 0EQ
West Yorkshire
England

Tel: 01274 307233
Fax: 01274 740698
Email: admin@alm.org.uk
Website: www.alm.org.uk